Dewey

Dewey

the Library Cat

A TRUE STORY

Vicki Myron

with

Bret Witter

Little, Brown and Company

New York Boston

Little, Brown and Company

Hachette Book Group
237 Park Avenue, New York, NY 10017
Visit our Web site at www.lb-kids.com

Little, Brown and Company is a division of Hachette Book Group, Inc.
The Little, Brown name and logo are trademarks of Hachette Book Group, Inc.

First Edition: May 2010

Library of Congress Cataloging-in-Publication Data

Myron, Vicki.
    Dewey the Library Cat: A True Story / Vicki Myron with Bret Witter.
       p. cm.
    ISBN 978-0-316-06871-0
    1. Dewey (Cat)—Juvenile literature.   2. Library cats—Iowa—Spencer—Biography—
Juvenile literature.   I. Witter, Bret.   II. Title.
    SF445.5.M972 2010
    636.8092'9—dc22

                                                                                            2009030867

10 9 8 7 6 5 4 3 2 1

RRD-C

Printed in the United States of America

Vicki—To Dewey, my Little Buddy

Bret—To Lydia and Isaac, as always

CONTENTS

CHAPTER 1

Lost and Found

Y ou find all kinds of things in a library book return box—garbage, snowballs, soda cans. Stick a hole in a wall and you're asking for trouble. I should know. My name is Vicki Myron, and I am the former director of the Spencer Public Library in Spencer, Iowa. At our library, the book return slot was in a back alley across the street from the town's middle school, so rocks and snowballs were the least of our worries. Several times we were startled in the middle of the day by a loud explosion from the back of the library. Inside the book return box, we'd find a firecracker.

After the weekend, the drop box would also be full of books, so every Monday morning I took them out of the box and loaded them onto one of our book carts. Same thing every week. Until one morning, one of the coldest mornings of the year, when I came in with the book cart and found Jean Hollis Clark, a fellow librarian, standing dead still in the middle of the staff room.

"I heard a noise from the drop box," Jean said.

"What kind of noise?"

"I think it's an animal."

"A what?"

"An animal," Jean said. "I think there's an animal in the drop box."

That was when I heard it, a low rumble from under the metal cover. It didn't sound like an animal. It sounded like an old man clearing his throat.

Gurr-gug-gug. Gurr-gug-gug.

But the opening at the top of the chute was only a few inches wide, so that would be quite a squeeze for an old man. It had to be an animal. But what kind? I got down on my knees, reached over to the lid, and hoped for a chipmunk.

What I got instead was a blast of freezing air. The night before, the temperature had reached minus fifteen degrees, and that didn't take into account the wind, which cut under your coat

2

and squeezed your bones. And on that night, of all nights, someone had jammed a book into the return slot, wedging it open. It was as cold in the box as it was outside, maybe colder, since the box was lined with metal. It was the kind of cold that made it almost painful to breathe.

I was still catching my breath, in fact, when I saw the kitten huddled in the front left corner of the box. It was tucked up in a little space underneath a book, so all I could see at first was its head. It looked gray in the shadows, almost like a little rock, and I could tell its fur was dirty and tangled. Carefully, I lifted the book. The kitten looked up at me, slowly and sadly, and for a second I looked straight into its huge golden eyes. Then it lowered its head and sank down into its hole.

At that moment, I lost every bone in my body and just melted.

The kitten wasn't trying to appear tough. It wasn't trying to hide. I don't even think it was scared. It was just hoping to be saved.

I lifted the kitten out of the box. It was so small that my hands nearly swallowed it. We found out later it was eight weeks old, but it looked like it was barely eight days old. It was so thin I could see every rib. I could feel its heart beating, its lungs pumping. The poor kitten was so weak it could barely hold up its head, and it was shaking uncontrollably. It opened its mouth, but the sound was weak and ragged.

And the cold! That's what I remember most, because I couldn't believe a living animal could be so cold. It felt like there was no warmth at all. So I cradled the kitten in my arms to share my heat. It didn't fight. Instead, it snuggled into my chest and laid its head against my heart.

"Oh, my," said Jean.

"The poor baby," I said, squeezing tighter.

Neither of us said anything for a while. We were just staring at the kitten.

Finally Jean broke the silence. "How do you think it got in there?"

I wasn't thinking about last night. I was only thinking about right now. It was too early to call the veterinarian, who wouldn't be in for an hour. But the kitten was so cold. Even in the warmth of my arms, I could feel it shaking.

"We've got to do something," I said.

Jean grabbed a towel, and we wrapped the little fellow up until only its pink nose was sticking out. Its huge beautiful eyes were staring from the shadows.

"Let's give it a warm bath," I said. "Maybe that will stop the shivering."

I filled the staff room sink with warm water, testing it with my elbow as I clutched the kitten in my arms. It slid into the sink like a block of ice. Jean found some shampoo in the art closet, and I rubbed the kitten slowly and lovingly. As the water turned grayer and grayer, the kitten's wild shivering turned to soft purring. I smiled. This kitten was tough. But it was so very young. When I finally lifted it out of the sink, it looked like a newborn: huge lidded eyes and big ears sticking out from a tiny head. Wet, scared, and meowing quietly for its mother.

We dried it with the blow-dryer we used for drying glue at craft time. Within thirty seconds, I was holding a beautiful, long-haired orange tabby. The kitten had been so filthy before, I had thought it was gray.

By this time there were four people in the staff room, each cooing over the kitten. Eight hands touched it, seemingly at once. The other three staffers talked over one another while I stood silently cradling the kitten like a baby and rocking back and forth.

"Where did it come from?"

"The drop box."

"No!"

"Is it a boy or a girl?"

I glanced up. They were all looking at me. "A boy," I said.

"He's beautiful."

"How old is he?"

"How did he get in the box?"

I wasn't listening. I only had eyes for the kitten.

"It's so cold."

"Bitterly cold."

"The coldest morning of the year."

A pause, then: "Someone must have put him in the box."

"That's awful."

"Maybe they were trying to save him."

"I don't know. He's so...helpless."

"He's so young."

"He's so beautiful. Oh, he's breaking my heart."

I put him down on the table. The poor kitten could barely stand. The pads on all four of his paws were frostbitten, and over the next week they would turn white and peel off. And yet the kitten managed to do something truly amazing. He steadied himself on the table and slowly looked up into each face. Then he began to hobble. As each librarian reached to pet him, he rubbed his tiny head against her hand and purred. It was as if he wanted to personally thank every person he met for saving his life.

By now it had been twenty minutes since I had pulled the tiny kitten out of the box, and I'd had plenty of time to think through a few things—the once common practice of keeping library cats, my plan to make the library more friendly, the logistics of bowls and food and cat litter, the trusting expression on the kitten's face when he burrowed into my chest and looked up into my eyes. So I was more than prepared when someone finally asked, "What should we do with him?"

"Well," I said, as if the thought had just occurred to me, "maybe we can keep him."

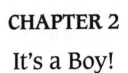

CHAPTER 2

It's a Boy!

The most amazing thing about the kitten was how happy he was that first day. Here he was in a new environment, surrounded by eager strangers who wanted nothing more than to squeeze him, cuddle him, and coo, and he was perfectly calm. No matter how many times we passed him from hand to hand, and no matter what position we held him in, he was never jumpy or fidgety. He never tried to bite or get away. Instead, he just relaxed into each person's arms and stared up into her eyes.

Can you imagine it, the tiniest ball of fluff in the world, no bigger than a juice box, staring up into your eyes with love? And then nuzzling you with his wet nose. And laying his head on your arm. And purring. No wonder we didn't want to put him down! All we wanted to do was grab him, hold him, and love him.

In fact, when I set him down at closing time that first night, I had to watch him for five minutes to make sure he could totter all the way to his food dish and litter box. If he was going to be a library cat, he had to learn to live in the library. If I took him home, even for one night, he might imprint on my home and never want to leave. So I had to leave him alone in the library that first night.

But he looked so tiny as he limped across that big library, like a little lopsided toy. And he looked like he was trying so hard. The poor guy. I don't think his frostbitten feet had touched the ground all day.

Still, I wasn't too worried about him. I'd taken him to the vet that morning, and he wasn't in any health danger. He was an alley cat, so he was used to being alone at night. And thanks to the librarians, he already had a box to sleep in and toys to play with.

One librarian, Doris Armstrong, had even brought him a warm pink blanket. We had all watched as she bent down and scratched the kitten under the chin, then folded the blanket and put it in his cardboard box. The kitten had stepped gingerly into the box, curled his legs underneath his body for warmth, and fallen asleep. And that's exactly where I found him the next morning, asleep on his warm pink blanket.

The next step was to share our little guy with the outside world. The library staff may have already accepted the kitten, but keeping him wasn't our decision. The Spencer Public Library was part of the city government, which meant it answered to the city council and the library board. But it also answered to the ten thousand people of Spencer, and they could be a pretty opinionated bunch. If we wanted to keep the kitten, we needed the library board to approve. But more than that, we needed the town to want him.

As a librarian, I know you can't just put any cute cat in a library. If he's not friendly, he's going to make enemies. If he's too shy or scared, nobody will stand up for him. If he's not patient, he's going to bite. If he's too rambunctious, he's going to make a mess.

I had no doubt about our boy. From the moment he looked up into my eyes, so calm and content, I knew he was perfect for the library. There wasn't a flutter in his heart as I held him in my arms; there wasn't a moment of panic in his eyes. He trusted me completely. He trusted everyone. That's what made him so special: his complete and unabashed trust. And because of it, I trusted him, too.

But that doesn't mean I wasn't a little apprehensive when I motioned Mary Huston, the town historian, into the staff area of the library. This was it: his first introduction to the public. As I took the kitten in my arms, I must admit that I felt a flutter in *my* heart. When the kitten had looked into my eyes, something had happened; we had made a connection. He was more than just a cat to me. It had only been a day, but already I couldn't stand the thought of being without him. What if Mary didn't like him?

"Why hello," Mary said with a smile when she saw the tiny kitten in my hands. She reached out to pet him on the top of the head—and he stretched out to sniff her hand!

"Oh, my," Mary said. "He's handsome."

Handsome. There was no other way to describe him. This was a handsome cat. His coat was a mix of vibrant orange and white with subtle darker stripes. It grew longer as he got older, but as a kitten it was thick and long only around his neck. A lot of cats have pointy noses, or their mouths jut out a bit too far, or they're a little lop-sided, but this kitten's face was perfect. And his eyes, those huge golden eyes!

But it wasn't just his looks that made him beautiful; it was also his personality. If you cared at all about cats, you just had to hold him. There was something in his face—in the way he looked at you—that called out for love.

"He likes to be cradled," I said, gently sliding him into Mary's arms. "On his back. Like a baby."

"A one-pound baby."

"I don't think he even weighs that much."

The kitten shook his tail and nestled down into Mary's arms.

"Oh, Vicki," Mary said. "He's adorable. What's his name?"

A good question, since he didn't actually have a name. I'd started calling him Dewey, but that was only because I had to call him something. Since he wasn't my cat, I didn't have the right to name him. The patrons of the library would get to do that...if they wanted us to keep him.

"We're calling him Dewey," I told Mary, "but that's just a nickname for now."

"Hi, Dewey," Mary said. "Do you like the library?"

Dewey stared into Mary's face, then nuzzled her arm with his head.

Mary looked up with a smile. "I could hold him all day."

But, of course, she didn't. She put Dewey back into my arms, and I took him around the corner. The entire staff was waiting for us.

"That went well," I said. "One person down, 9,999 people to go."

CHAPTER 3

Purr-fect Addition

Slowly, we started introducing Dewey to more regular visitors who loved cats. He was still weak, so we passed him directly into their arms. Marcie Muckey was instantly smitten. Mike Baehr and his wife, Peg, loved him. Pat Jones and Judy Johnson thought he was adorable. Actually there were four Judy Johnsons among the ten thousand people in Spencer. Two were regular library users, and both were Dewey fans.

A week later, Dewey's story ran on the front page of the *Spencer Daily Reporter* under the headline "Purr-fect Addition Made to Spencer Library." The article, which took up half the page, told the story of Dewey's miraculous rescue and was accompanied by a color photo-graph of a tiny orange kitten staring shyly but confidently into the camera from atop an old-fashioned pull-drawer card catalog.

For a week, Dewey had been a secret. If you didn't come into the library, you didn't know about him. Now everyone in town knew. Many people, especially children, loved the idea of having a cat in the library. Most people didn't give Dewey a second thought.

But there were some complainers. I was a little disappointed, I must admit, but not surprised. There is nothing on earth that someone won't complain about.

One woman took particular offense. She sent me a letter that was pure fire and brimstone. According to her, I was a madwoman who was not only threatening the health of every inno-cent child in town, but also destroying the val-ues of the community. An animal! In a library! If we let that stand, what was to stop people from walking a cow down Grand Avenue? In fact, she threatened to show up in the library that very afternoon with her cow on a leash.

But you know what? I looked up her name in our files. She'd never checked a book out from the library. Never. In fact, she didn't even have a library card!

But I did get some worried phone calls. "My child has allergies," one woman said. "What am I going to do? He loves the library."

I knew allergies would be the most common concern, so I was prepared. A year earlier, Muffin, the beloved cat-in-residence at the Putnam Valley Library in upstate New York, had been banished after a library board member developed a severe cat allergy. As a consequence, the library lost $80,000 in promised donations. I had no intention of letting my cat, or my library, go the way of Muffin.

Spencer was too small for an allergist, so I asked the advice of two general practice doctors. The Spencer Public Library, they noted, was a large, open space sectioned off by rows of four-foot-high shelves. The staff area was enclosed by a temporary wall, leaving six feet open to the ceiling. There were two door-size openings in that wall, and since neither had a door, they were always open. Even the staff area was an open space, with desks pushed back-to-back or separated by bookshelves.

Not only did this layout allow Dewey easy

access to the safety of the staff area, but the doctors assured me it would also prevent the buildup of dander and hair. The library, apparently, was perfectly designed to prevent allergies. If anyone on staff had been allergic it might have been a problem, but a few hours of exposure every couple of days? The doctors agreed there was nothing to worry about.

The parents were skeptical, but most brought their children to the library for a trial run. I held Dewey in my arms for each visit. I didn't know how the parents would react or how Dewey would respond because the children were so excited to see him. Their mothers and fathers would tell them to be gentle. The children would approach slowly and whisper, "Hi, Dewey," and then explode with squeals as their parents ushered them away with a quick, "That's enough." Dewey didn't mind the noise; he was the calmest kitten I'd ever seen. He did mind, I think, that these children weren't allowed to pet him.

But a few days later, one family came back with a camera. And this time the allergic little boy was sitting beside Dewey, petting him, while his mother took pictures.

"Justin can't have pets," she told me. "I never

knew how much he missed them. He loves Dewey already."

I loved Dewey already, too. We all loved Dewey. How could you resist his charm? He was affectionate, social, beautiful—and still limping on his tiny frostbitten feet.

What I couldn't believe was how much Dewey loved us. How comfortable he seemed around strangers. His attitude seemed to be *How can anyone resist me?* I soon realized that Dewey didn't think of himself as just another cat.

He always thought of himself, correctly, as one of a kind.

CHAPTER 4

Dewey Readmore Books

Dewey was a lucky cat. He not only survived the freezing library drop box, but also fell into the arms of a staff that loved him and a library perfectly designed to care for him. There were no two ways about it, Dewey led a charmed life. But Spencer was also lucky, because Dewey couldn't have fallen into our lives at a better time. That winter wasn't just cold; it was one of the worst times in Spencer's history.

Spencer was a farming town. For miles around, all you could see were farms. But in the 1980s, there was a farm crisis. Land was too expensive, crop prices were too cheap, and farms started to go out of business. When the farmers couldn't pay their loans, the banks failed. Then the stores closed because there was nobody to buy their goods. People lost their jobs. More farms closed. After a while, it felt like the whole region was being pulled steadily down. There was even a running joke: The last store owner out of downtown Spencer, please turn off the lights.

Then into our lives came Dewey. I don't want to make too much of that, because Dewey didn't put food on anyone's table. He didn't create jobs. He didn't turn our economy around. Dewey was a welcome distraction.

But he was so much more, too. Dewey's story resonated with the people of Spencer. Here was an alley cat, left for dead in a freezing drop box, terrified, alone, and clinging to life. He made it through that dark night, and that terrible event turned out to be the best thing that ever happened to him. He never lost his trust, no matter what the circumstances, or his appreciation for life. From the moment we found him, Dewey believed everything was going to be fine.

And when he was around, he made others believe that, too. It took him ten days to get healthy enough to explore the library on his own, and once he did, it was clear he had no interest in books and shelves. His interest was people. If there was a patron in the library, he'd walk straight up to her—still slow on his sore feet—and jump into her lap. Often he was pushed away, but rejection never deterred him. Dewey kept jumping, kept looking for laps to lie in and hands to pet him, and things started to change.

I noticed it first with the older patrons, who often came to the library to flip through magazines or browse for books. Once Dewey started spending time with them, they showed up more frequently and stayed longer. The ones who had always given the staff a friendly wave or good morning now engaged us in conversation, and that conversation was usually about Dewey. They couldn't get enough Dewey stories. They weren't just filling their time now; they were visiting friends.

One older man in particular came in at the same time every morning, sat in the same big, comfortable chair, and read the newspaper. His wife had recently passed away, and he was lonely. I didn't expect him to be a cat person, but from the first moment Dewey climbed into his lap, the man was beaming. Suddenly he wasn't reading the newspaper alone anymore.

"Are you happy here, Dewey?" the man would ask every morning as he petted his new friend. Dewey would shut his eyes and, more often than not, drop off to sleep.

And then there was the man looking for a job. I didn't know him, but I knew his type—proud, hardworking, probably a father with kids at home—and I knew he was suffering. He was from Spencer, a laborer, not a farmer. His job-hunting outfit, like his former work outfit, was jeans and a regular shirt. Every morning, Dewey approached him, and every morning the man pushed him away. Then one day I saw Dewey sitting on his lap, and for the first time in weeks, the man was smiling. There was still sadness in his eyes, but he was smiling.

Maybe Dewey couldn't give much, but in the winter of 1988 he gave exactly what Spencer needed. So I gave our kitten to the town. The staff understood. He wasn't our cat. He belonged to the patrons of the Spencer Public Library. I put a box by the front door and told people, "You know the cat who sits on your lap? The one who reads the newspaper with you? Who steals the lipstick out of your purse and knocks your pencils to the ground? Well, he's your cat, and I want you to help name him."

I had been library director for only six months, so I was still enthusiastic about contests. Every few weeks we put a box in the lobby, made an announcement on the local radio station, and offered a prize for the winning entry. A good contest with a good prize might draw fifty entries. If the prize was expensive, like a television set, we might scrape up seventy. Usually we got about twenty-five.

Our Name the Kitty contest, which wasn't mentioned on the radio because I wanted only regular patrons to participate, and didn't even offer a prize, received 397 entries. Three hundred ninety-seven entries! That's when I realized the library had stumbled onto something important. Community interest in Dewey was off all our charts!

Lasagna-loving Garfield was at the height of his popularity, so Garfield was a popular name choice. There were nine votes for Tiger. Tigger was almost as popular. Morris was another multiple vote-getter. Even cultural blips like ALF (a cuddly alien puppet with his own television show) and Spuds (after Spuds MacKenzie, a dog in television commercials) received votes. There were a few mean-spirited entries, like Fleabag, and some that were just plain weird, like Cat-gang Amadeus Taffy (a sudden sweet tooth?), Ladybooks (an odd name for a boy), Hop-snopper, Boxcar, and Nukster.

By far the most entries, more than fifty, were for Dewey. Apparently the patrons had already grown attached to this kitten, and they didn't want him to change. Not even his name. And to be honest, the staff didn't, either. We, too, had grown attached to Dewey just the way he was.

Still, the name needed something. So we decided to think of a last name. Mary Walk, our children's librarian, suggested Readmore. A commercial running during the Saturday morning cartoons—this was back when cartoons were only shown before noon on Saturdays, if you can believe it—featured a cartoon cat named O. G. Readmore who encouraged kids to "read a book and take a look at the TV in your head." I'm sure that's where the name came from.

Dewey Readmore. Hmmm. Close, but not quite. I suggested the last name Books.

Dewey Readmore Books. One name for the

librarians, who live by the Dewey decimal system. One for the children, who loved cartoons. One for the written word.

Do We Read More Books? A challenge to be well-read. A name to put us in the mood to learn.

Dewey Readmore Books. Three names for our regal, confident, beautiful cat. I'm sure we'd have named him Sir Dewey Readmore Books if we had thought of it, but we were librarians; we didn't stand on pomp and circumstance. And neither did Dewey. He always went by his first name or, occasionally, just "the Dew."

CHAPTER 5

The Dewey Carry

Cats are creatures of habit, and it didn't take long for Dewey to develop a routine. When I arrived at the library every morning, he was waiting for me at the front door. He would take a few bites of his food while I hung up my jacket and bag, and then we would walk the library together, making sure everything was in place and discussing our evenings. Dewey was more a sniffer than a talker, but I didn't mind.

After our walk, Dewey would visit the staff. If someone was having a bad morning, he'd spend extra time with her. He had an amazing sense of who needed him, and he was always willing to give his time. But never for too long. At two minutes to nine, Dewey would drop whatever he was doing and race for the front door.

A patron was always waiting outside at exactly nine o'clock when we opened the doors, and she would usually enter with a warm, "Hi, Dewey. How are you this morning?"

Welcome, welcome, I imagined him saying from his post to the left of the door. *Why don't you pet the cat?*

No response. The early birds were usually there for a reason, which meant they didn't have time to stop for a cat.

No petting? Fine. There's always another person where you came from—wherever that is.

It wouldn't take long for him to find a lap, and since he'd been up for two hours that usually meant it was time for a nap. Dewey was already so comfortable in the library he had no problem falling asleep in public places. He could fall asleep anywhere.

Dewey preferred laps for naps, but if they weren't available he would curl up in a box. The cards for the catalog came in small boxes about the size of a pair of baby shoes. Dewey liked to cram all four feet inside, sit down, and let his sides ooze over the edge. If he found a bigger box, he buried his head and tail in the bottom. The only thing you could see was a big blob of back fur sticking out of the top. He looked like a muffin.

Once, I watched him slowly wind his way into a half-empty tissue box. He put his two front feet through the slit on top, then delicately stepped in with the other two. Slowly he sat down on his hind legs and rolled his back end until it was wedged into the box. Then he started bending his front legs and working the front of his body into the crease. The operation took four or five minutes, but finally there was nothing left but his head sticking out in one direction and his tail sticking out in the other. He just stared into the distance, pretending the rest of the world didn't exist.

In those days, Iowa provided envelopes with its tax forms, and we always put a box of them out for patrons. Dewey must have spent half his first winter curled up in that box.

"I need an envelope," a patron would say nervously, "but I don't want to disturb Dewey. What should I do?"

"Don't worry. He's asleep."

"But won't it wake him up? He's lying on top of them."

"Oh, no, the Dew's dead to the world."

The patron would gently roll Dewey to the side and then, far more carefully than necessary, slide out an envelope. He could have jerked it like a magician pulling a tablecloth from under a dinner setting, it wouldn't have mattered. Dewey was an expert when it came to napping.

"Cat hair comes with the envelope," I'd say. "No charge."

Dewey's other favorite resting spot was the back of the copier.

"Don't worry," I told the confused patrons, "you can't disturb him. He sleeps there because it's warm. The more copies you make, the more heat the machine produces, and the happier he'll be."

The staff, meanwhile, had no such hesitation when it came to the Dew. One of my first decisions was that no library funds, not one penny, would ever be spent on Dewey's care. Instead, we kept a Dewey Box in the back room. Everyone on staff tossed in their loose change. Most of us also brought in soda cans. Cynthia Behrends would take the cans to a recycling drop-off every week and exchange them for a few dollars. The whole staff was feeding our kitty.

In return for these small contributions, we'd get endless hours of pleasure. Dewey loved drawers, and he developed a habit of popping out of them and scaring the pants off us. If you were shelving books, he'd jump onto the cart and demand a trip around the library. And when Kim Peterson, the library secretary, started typing, you knew a show was about to begin. As soon as I heard those keys, I'd put down my work and wait for the signal.

"Dewey's after the clacker thingies again!" Kim would call out.

I'd hurry out of my office to find Dewey hunched on the back of Kim's big white typewriter. His head would be jerking from side to side as the disk moved left to right, then back again, until finally he couldn't take it anymore and lunged at the "clacker thingies," which were the keys rising up to strike the paper. The whole staff would be there, watching and laughing. Dewey's antics always drew a crowd.

But no matter how much fun Dewey was having, he never forgot his routine. At exactly ten thirty, he would hop up and head for the staff room. Jean ate yogurt on her break, and if he hung around long enough, she'd let him lick the lid. Jean was quiet and hardworking, but she always found ways to accommodate Dewey. If Dewey wanted downtime, he would lie limply over Jean's left shoulder—and only her left shoulder, never her right.

After a few months, when Dewey wouldn't let us hold him cradled in our arms anymore (too much like a baby, I guess), the whole staff adopted Jean's over-the-shoulder technique. We called it the Dewey Carry.

CHAPTER 6

Dewey's Least Favorite Things

Dewey helped me with downtime, too, which was nice, since I had a tendency to work too hard. Many days I'd be hunched over my desk for hours, so intent on my work that I wouldn't even realize Dewey was there until he sprang into my lap.

"How you doing, baby boy?" I'd say with a smile. "So nice to see you."

I'd pet him a few times before turning back to my work. Unsatisfied, he'd climb on my desk and start sniffing.

"Oh, you just happened, *accidentally*, to sit on the paper I'm working on, didn't you?"

I'd put him on the floor. He'd hop back up.

"Not now, Dewey. I'm busy." I'd put him back down.

He'd hop back up.

Maybe if I ignore him, I'd think, *he'll lose interest.*

Nope. Dewey would push his head against my pencil.

I'd push him aside.

Fine, he'd think, *I'll knock these pens to the ground.* Which he proceeded to do, one pen at a time. I couldn't help but laugh.

"Okay, Dewey, you win." I'd wad up a piece of paper and throw it to him. He'd run after it, sniff it, then come back. Typical cat.

I'd walk over, pick up the paper, and toss it a few more times.

"What am I going to do with you?"

But it wasn't all jokes and games. I was the boss, and I had responsibilities—like giving the cat a bath. The first time I bathed Dewey, I was confident things would go well. He loved the bath that first morning, right?

This time, Dewey slid calmly into the sink... and completely freaked out as soon as he touched the water. He thrashed. He screamed. He put his feet on the edge of the sink and tried to throw his body over the side. What did he think, all that water was going to melt him? Twenty minutes later, both of us were soaking wet and exhausted. Dewey's fur was twisted up in knots. My hair looked like I had stuck my tongue in a light socket. Everybody laughed.

The next bath was just as bad. I managed to get Dewey scrubbed, but I didn't have the patience for toweling and blow-drying. Not this crazy kitten.

"Fine," I told him. "If you hate it that much, just go."

Dewey was a vain cat. He would spend an hour washing his face. The funniest part was the way he would ball up his fist, lick it, and shove it into his ears. He would work those ears until they were sparkling white. Now, soaking wet, he looked like a some sort of hairy sea creature that had washed up on the beach. It was pathetic. The staff was laughing and taking pictures, but Dewey looked so genuinely upset that after a few minutes the pictures stopped.

"Have a sense of humor, Dew," I teased him. "You brought this on yourself."

He curled up behind a shelf of books and didn't come out for hours. After that, Dewey and I agreed that two baths a year were plenty.

"If you thought the bath was bad," I told Dewey a few months into his stay at the library, "you're not going to like this at all." I wrapped him in his green towel and brought him to the car.

Five minutes later, we arrived at Dr. Esterly's office. There were several veterinarians in Spencer—after all, we lived in an area prone to breech-birth cows, distressed hogs, and sick farm dogs—but I preferred Dr. Esterly. He was a quiet, modest man with an extremely deliberate way of speaking. His voice was deep and slow like a lazy river, and he didn't rush. He was a big man but his hands were gentle. And he loved animals.

"Hi, Dewey," he said, checking him over.

I looked down at Dewey's tiny paws, which had finally healed. There were tufts of fur sticking out from between his toes. "Do you think he's part Persian?"

Dr. Esterley looked at Dewey. His regal bearing. The glorious ruff of long orange fur around his neck.

"No. He's just a good-looking alley cat."

I didn't believe it for a second.

He was a lion in alley cat clothing.

"Dewey is a product of survival of the fittest,"

35

Dr. Esterly continued. "His ancestors have probably lived in that alley for generations."

"So he's one of us."

Dr. Esterly smiled. "I suppose so. You'll just need to leave him with me overnight."

"Do you think this is absolutely necessary, Doctor?"

"Cats need to be neutered," he said as he picked Dewey up and held him under his arm.

Dewey was relaxed and purring. The last thing Dr. Esterly said before they disappeared around the corner was, "Dewey is one fine cat."

He sure was. And I missed him already.

When I picked Dewey up the next morning, my heart almost broke in two. He had a faraway look in his eyes, and a little shaved belly. I took him in my arms. He pushed his head against me and started purring. He was so happy to see his old pal Vicki.

Back at the library, the staff dropped everything. "Poor baby. Poor baby," they said. I gave him over to their care—Dewey was with friends, after all—and went back to work. One more set of hands and he might be crushed. Besides, the trip to the vet's office had put me behind, and I had a mountain of work.

But I wasn't alone for long. An hour later, as I was hanging up the phone, I looked up to see Dewey hobbling through my office door. I knew he'd been getting love and attention from the rest of the staff, but I could tell from his determined wobbling that he needed something more.

Sure, cats can be fun, but my relationship with Dewey was already far more. He was so intelligent. He was so playful. He treated people so well. I didn't yet have as deep a bond with him as I would later, but already I loved him.

And he loved me back. Not like he loved everyone else, but in a special and deeper way. The look he gave me that first morning meant something. It really did. Never was that more clear than now, as he pushed toward me with such determination. I could almost hear him saying, *Where have you been? I missed you.*

I reached down, scooped him up, and cradled him against my chest. I don't know if I said it out loud or to myself, but it didn't matter. Dewey could already read my moods. "I'm your mama, aren't I?"

Dewey put his head on my shoulder, right up against my neck, and purred.

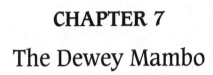

CHAPTER 7

The Dewey Mambo

Don't get me wrong, everything wasn't perfect with the Dew. Yes, he was a sweet and beautiful cat, and yes, he was extraordinarily trusting and generous, but he was still a kitten. He'd streak crazily through the staff room. He'd knock your work to the floor out of pure playfulness. Sometimes he wouldn't take no for an answer when a patron wanted to be left alone. At Story Hour, his presence would make the children so rambunctious that Mary Walk, our children's librarian, banned him from the room.

Then there was Mark, a large fabric puppet of a child with muscular dystrophy that we used to teach schoolchildren about disabilities. Every night, Dewey would sleep on the puppet. There was so much cat hair on Mark's legs that we finally had to put him in a closet. Dewey worked all night until he figured out how to open that closet, then he went right back to sleeping on Mark's lap. We bought a lock for the closet the next day.

But nothing compared to his behavior around catnip. Doris Armstrong was always bringing Dewey presents, such as little balls or toy mice. Doris had cats of her own, and she always thought of Dewey when she went to the pet store for their litter and food. One day near the end of Dewey's first summer, she quite innocently brought in a bag of fresh catnip. Dewey was so excited by the smell I thought he was going to climb her leg. For the first time in his life, the cat actually begged.

When Doris finally crumbled a few leaves on the floor, Dewey went crazy. He started smelling them so hard I thought he was going to inhale the floor. After a few sniffs, he started sneezing, but he didn't slow down. Instead, he started chewing the leaves, then alternating back and forth: chewing, sniffing, chewing, sniffing.

His muscles started to ripple, a slow cascade of tension flowing out of his bones and down his back.

When he finally shook that tension out the end of his tail, he flopped over on the ground and rolled back and forth in the catnip. He rolled until he lost every bone in his body. Unable to walk, he slithered on the floor, undulating as he rubbed his chin along the carpet like a snow-plow blade. I mean, the cat oozed.

Then, gradually, Dewey's spine bent back-ward, in slow motion, until his head was resting on his behind. Cat-bent-in-half. But he didn't stop there. He formed figure eights, zigzags, pret-zels. I swear the front half of his body wasn't even connected to the back half. We called it the Dewey Mambo.

When he accidentally ended up flat on his tummy, he rippled his way back to the catnip and started rolling in it all over again. Eventually, Dewey rolled over onto his back, lifted his back legs, and started kicking himself in the chin. The kicks started out fast, but they got slower and slower and slower until, finally, with a few weak kicks hanging feebly in the air, Dewey fell asleep right on top of the last of the catnip. My goodness, it was funny!

Dewey never tired of catnip. And every time he got hold of some, it was the same thing: the Dewey Mambo, the chin kicks, and then, finally, one very tired cat fast asleep on the library floor.

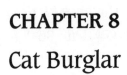

CHAPTER 8

Cat Burglar

Dewey's other major interest—besides people, puppets, drawers, boxes, copiers, typewriters, and catnip—was rubber bands. Dewey was absolutely fanatical about rubber bands. He didn't even need to see them; he could smell them across the library. As soon as you put a box of rubber bands on your desk, he was there.

"Here you go, Dewey," I would say as I opened a new bag. "One for you and one for me." He would take his rubber band in his mouth and happily skip away.

I would find it the next morning...you know, in his...litter box. It looked like a worm poking its head out of a chunk of dirt. I thought, *That can't be good.*

I decided to address this at our staff meeting. Dewey always attended the meetings, but fortunately he wasn't able to understand what we were talking about. So I ended the meeting with a gentle reminder: "Don't give Dewey any more rubber bands. I don't care how much he begs. He's been eating them, and I have a feeling rubber isn't the healthiest food for a growing kitten."

The next day, there were more rubber band worms in Dewey's litter. And the next. And the next.

At the next staff meeting, I was more direct. "Is anyone giving Dewey rubber bands?"

No. No. No. No. No.

"Then he must be stealing them. From now on, don't leave rubber bands lying out on your desk."

Easier said than done. Much, much easier said than done. You would be amazed how many rubber bands there are in a library. We all put our rubber band holders away, but that didn't even dent the problem. Rubber bands are sneaky critters. They slide under computer keyboards and crawl into your pencil holder. They fall under your desk and hide in the wires. One evening I even caught Dewey rummaging through a stack of work on someone's desk. There was a rubber band lurking every time he pushed a piece of paper aside.

"Even the hidden ones need to go," I said at the next staff meeting. "Let's clean up those desks and put them away. Remember, Dewey can *smell* rubber." In just a few days, the staff area looked neater than it had in years.

So Dewey started raiding the rubber bands left on the circulation desk for patrons. We stashed them in a drawer. He found the rubber bands by the copier, too. Those went into another drawer. The patrons were just going to have to ask for rubber bands. A small price to pay, I thought, for a cat that spent most of his day trying to make them happy.

Soon, our rubber band operation was showing signs of success. There were still rubber worms in the litter box but not nearly as many. And Dewey was being forced into brazenness. Every time I pulled out a rubber band, he was watching me.

"Getting desperate, are we?"

As soon as I put the rubber band down, Dewey pounced. I pushed him away; he sat on the desk waiting for his chance. "Not this time, Dewey," I said with a grin. I admit, this game was fun.

Dewey became more subtle. He waited for you to turn your back, then pounced on the rubber band left innocently lying on your desk. It had been there five minutes. Humans forget. Not cats. Dewey remembered every drawer left open a crack, then came back that night to wiggle his way inside. He never messed up the contents of the drawer. The next morning, the rubber bands were simply gone.

One afternoon I was walking past our big floor-to-ceiling supply cabinet. I was focused on something else, and only noticed the open door out of the corner of my eye. "Did I just see..."

I turned around and walked back to the cabinet. Sure enough, there was Dewey, sitting on a shelf, a huge rubber band hanging out of his mouth.

You can't stop the Dew! I'm going to be feasting for a week.

I had to laugh. In general, Dewey was the best-behaved kitten I had ever seen. He never knocked books or displays off shelves. If I told him not to do something, he usually stopped. He was unfailingly kind to strangers and staffers alike. For a kitten, he was downright mellow. But he was absolutely incorrigible when it came to rubber bands. The cat would go anywhere and do anything to sink his teeth into a rubber band.

"Hold on, Dewey," I told him, putting down my pile of work. "I'm going to get a picture of this." By the time I got back with the camera, the cat and his rubber band were gone.

"Make sure all the cabinets and drawers are completely closed," I reminded the staff. Dewey was already notorious. He had a habit of getting closed inside cabinets and then leaping out at the next person to open them. We weren't sure if it was a game or an accident, but Dewey clearly enjoyed it.

A few mornings later I found file cards sitting unbound on the front desk. Dewey had never gone for tight rubber bands before; now, he started biting them off every night. As always, he was delicate even in defiance. He left perfectly neat stacks, not a card out of place. The cards went into the drawers; the drawers were shut tight.

After nine months, you could spend an entire day in the Spencer Public Library without seeing a rubber band. Oh, they were still there, but they were hidden away where only those with opposable thumbs could get to them. It was the ultimate cleaning operation. The library looked beautiful; we were proud. There was just one problem: Dewey was still chewing rubber bands.

I put together an investigative team. It took us two days to find Dewey's last good source: the coffee mug on Mary Walk's desk.

"Mary," I said, flipping a notebook like the police detective in a bad television drama, "we have reason to believe the rubber bands are coming from your mug."

"That's impossible. I've never seen Dewey around my desk."

"Evidence suggests the suspect is intentionally avoiding your desk to throw us off the trail. We believe he only approaches the mug at night."

"What evidence?"

I pointed to several small pieces of chewed rubber band on the floor. "He chews them up and spits them out. He eats them for breakfast. I think you know all the usual clichés."

Mary shuddered at the thought of the garbage on the floor having passed into and out of the stomach of a cat. Still, it seemed so improbable...

"The mug is six inches deep. It's full of paper clips, staples, pens, pencils. How could he possibly pluck out rubber bands without knocking everything over?"

"Where there's a will, there's a way. And this suspect has proven, in all his months at the library, that he has the will."

"But there are hardly any rubber bands in there! Surely this isn't his only source!"

"How about an experiment? You put the mug in the cabinet, we'll see if he pukes rubber bands in the morning."

"But this mug has my children's pictures on it!"

"Good point. How about we just remove the rubber bands?"

Mary decided to put a lid on the mug. The next morning, the lid was on her desk with teeth marks along one edge. No doubt about it, the mug was the source. The rubber bands went into a drawer. Convenience was sacrificed for the greater good.

We never completely succeeded in wiping out Dewey's rubber band fixation—or his supply. He'd lose interest, only to go back on the prowl a few months or even a few years later. In the end, it was more a game than a battle, a contest of wits versus will. We had the wits; Dewey had the will. And he had that powerful, rubber-sniffing nose.

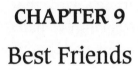

CHAPTER 9

Best Friends

Now let's not make too much of this. Rubber bands were a hobby, that's all. Catnip and boxes were mere distractions. Dewey's true love was people, and there was nothing he wouldn't do for his adoring public.

I remember standing at the circulation desk one morning talking with Doris when we noticed a toddler wobbling by. She must have learned to walk recently, because her balance was shaky and her steps uneven. It wasn't helping that her arms were wrapped tightly across her chest, clutching Dewey in a bear hug. His rear and tail were sticking up in her face, and his head was hanging down toward the floor. Doris and

I stopped talking and watched in amazement as the little girl toddled in slow motion across the library, a very big smile on her face and a very resigned cat hanging upside down from her arms.

"Amazing," Doris said.

"I should do something about that," I said. But I didn't. I knew Dewey was in control of the situation. No matter what happened, he could take care of himself.

And besides, he had the whole library wrapped around his paw. When regular patrons came in and Dewey wasn't there to greet them, they'd go looking for him. That's the subtle difference between a cat and a dog, my friends: A dog finds you; a cat waits for you to find them.

First patrons searched the floor, figuring Dewey was hiding around a corner. Then they checked the top of the bookshelves. "Oh, how are you, Dewey? I didn't see you there," they would say, reaching up to pet him.

Dewey would give them the top of his head to pet, that's all. But as soon as they forgot about him, Dewey jumped into their laps. That's when I saw the smiles. By the end of his first year, dozens of patrons were telling me, "I know Dewey likes everyone, but I have a special relationship with him."

I smiled and nodded. *That's right, Judy,* I thought. *You and everyone else who comes into this library.*

Dewey's real favorites, though, were the children. If you wanted to understand the effect Dewey had on Spencer, all you had to do was look at the children. The smiles when they came into the library, the joy as they searched and called for him, the excitement when they found him.

The children wanted his attention, a fact that became very noticeable during Story Hour. Every Tuesday morning, the murmur of excited children in the Round Room, where Story Hour was held, would be suddenly punctuated by a cry of "Dewey's here!" A mad rush would ensue as every child in the room tried to pet Dewey at the same time.

"If you don't settle down," our children's librarian, Mary Walk, would tell them, "Dewey has to go."

A barely contained hush would fall over the room as the children took their seats, trying their best to contain their excitement. When they were relatively calm, Dewey would begin sliding between them, rubbing against each child and making them all giggle. Soon kids were grabbing at him and whispering, "Sit with me, Dewey. Sit with me."

"Children, don't make me warn you again."

"Yes, Mary." The children always called the librarians by their first names.

Dewey, knowing he had pushed the limit, would stop wandering and curl up in the lap of one lucky child. He didn't let a child grab him and hold him; he *chose* someone. And every week it was a different child.

Once he had chosen a lap, Dewey usually sat quietly for the whole hour. Unless a movie was being shown. Then he would jump on a table, curl his legs under his body, and watch the screen intently. When the credits rolled he'd feign boredom and jump down. Before the children could ask "Where's Dewey?", he was gone.

Dewey also won over the older kids. Spencer Middle School was across the street from the library, and about fifty students stayed with us after school while their parents were working. On the days they blew in like a hurricane, Dewey avoided them, especially the rowdy ones who pretended to be too cool for things like cats. But on calmer days he would mingle.

He had many friends among the students, both boys and girls. They petted him and played games with him, like rolling pencils off the table and watching his surprise when they disappeared. One girl would wiggle a pen out the end of her coat sleeve. Dewey would chase the pen up into the sleeve and then, deciding he liked that warm, dark, tight place, he'd sometimes lie down for a nap. Only his head would be sticking out, sort of like a hot dog peeking out from the end of a bun.

There was one child, though, Dewey couldn't win over. She was four years old when Dewey arrived, and she came to the library every week with her mother and older brother. Her brother loved Dewey, but she hung back as far as possible, looking tense and nervous. Her mother eventually confided in me that the girl was afraid of all four-legged animals, especially cats and dogs.

What an opportunity! I knew Dewey could do for this girl what he had done for the children with cat allergies who finally had a cat to spend time with. I suggested exposing her gently to

Dewey, first by looking through the window at him and then with supervised meetings.

"This is an ideal job for our gentle, loving Dewey," I told her mother. I was so enthusiastic, I even researched the best books to help the girl overcome her fear.

Her mother didn't want to go that route, so instead of trying to change the girl's feelings about cats, I accommodated her. When the girl came to the door and waved at the clerk at the front desk, we found Dewey and locked him in my office. Dewey hated being locked in my office, especially when patrons were in the library. *You don't have to do this,* I could hear him howling. *I know who she is! I won't go near her!*

I hated to lock him away, and I hated to miss the opportunity for Dewey to make this little girl's life better, but what could I do? *Don't force it, Vicki,* I told myself. *It will come.*

With that in mind I planned a low-key celebration for Dewey's first birthday: just a cake made out of cat food for Dewey, and a normal one for the patrons. We didn't know exactly when he was born, but Dr. Esterly had estimated he was eight weeks old when we found him, so we counted back to late November and chose the eighteenth. We had found Dewey on January 18, so we figured that was his lucky day.

A week before the celebration, we put out a card for signatures. Within days there were more than a hundred. At the next Story Hour, the children colored pictures of birthday cakes. Four days before the party, we strung the pictures on a clothesline behind the circulation desk. Then the newspaper ran a story, and we started receiving birthday cards in the mail. I couldn't believe it—people were sending birthday cards to a cat!

By the time the party rolled around, the kids were jumping up and down with excitement. Another cat would have been frightened, no doubt, but Dewey took it all in with his usual calm. Instead of interacting with the kids, though, he kept his eyes on the prize: his cat-food cake in the shape of a mouse, covered with Jean Hollis Clark's brand of full-fat yogurt (Dewey hated the diet stuff). As the kids smiled and giggled, I looked out at the parents gathered at the back of the crowd. They were smiling as much as the children.

DEWEY'S LIKES AND DISLIKES

(WRITTEN ON A BIG ORANGE POSTER BOARD FOR DEWEY'S FIRST BIRTHDAY ON NOVEMBER 18)

CATEGORY	♥ ♥ LOVES ♥ ♥	✖ ✖ HATES ✖ ✖
FOOD	Purina Special Dinners, Dairy Flavor	Anything else!
PLACE TO SLEEP	Any box or lap	Alone or in his own basket
TOY	Anything with catnip	Toys that don't move
TIME OF DAY	8:00 a.m. when the staff arrives	When everybody leaves
BODY POSITION	Stretched out on his back	Standing up for very long
TEMPERATURE	Warm, warm, warm	Cold, cold, cold
HIDING PLACE	Between the Westerns on the bottom shelf	The lobby
ACTIVITY	Making new friends, watching the copier	Going to the vet
PETTING	On the head, behind his ears	Scratched or touched on his stomach
EQUIPMENT	Kim's typewriter, the copier	Vacuum cleaner
ANIMAL	Himself!	None
GROOMING	Cleaning his ears	Being brushed or combed
MEDICINE	Felaxin (for hair balls)	Anything else
GAME	Hide-and-seek, pushing pen on the floor	Wrestling
PEOPLE	Almost everyone	People who are mean to him
NOISE	A snack being opened, paper rustling	Loud trucks, construction, dogs barking
BOOK	*The Cat Who Would Be King*	*101 Uses for a Dead Cat*

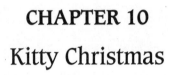

CHAPTER 10

Kitty Christmas

Shortly after Dewey's birthday, it was time for what would become his favorite holiday: Christmas. Now Christmas, you have to understand, was a holiday the town of Spencer celebrated together. The season started on the first weekend in December with the Grand Meander, a walking tour of Grand Avenue.

The street was strung with white lights; Christmas music was piped in; Santa Claus came to receive wish lists from the children (yes, even in the bad years he made it). The whole town was out, laughing, talking, and clutching one another to share the warmth. The stores stayed open late, showing off their holiday selections and offering cookies and hot chocolate to fight off the biting cold.

Every storefront window was decorated. We called them Living Windows, because in each one local residents acted out holiday scenes. The Parker Museum always created a vision of a pioneer Christmas. Other windows showcased the 1950s (my childhood!), with Radio Flyers and hula hoops. Some had mangers. Others featured toy tractors and cars for a boy's view of Christmas morning, or porcelain dolls for a girl's.

On the corner of First Avenue and Fifth Street, at the end of the Great Meander walk, the Festival of Trees, a Christmas tree decorating contest, was held. Since this was Dewey's first Christmas in Spencer, the library had entered a tree under the title "Do-We Love Christmas?" The tree was decorated with—what else?—pictures of Dewey. It also featured puffy kitten ornaments and garlands of red yarn. The presents under the tree were books like *The Cat-a-log* and *The Cat in the Hat*, tied in neat red bows. There was no official judging, but I think "Do-We Love Christmas?" was the winning Christmas tree that year, hands down.

But for Dewey, the real celebration began the next day in the library.

Every year, on the Monday after the Grand Meander, I took the Christmas decorations down from the top shelves of the library storage room. Cynthia Behrends and I always arrived early to set up and decorate the most important part: our big artificial Christmas tree. Cynthia was the hardest worker on staff and eagerly volunteered for every job. But she didn't know what she was getting into because this year, when we slid the long thin Christmas tree box off its high shelf, we had company.

"Dewey's excited this morning," she said. "He must like the looks of this box."

"Or the smell of all those plastic branches."

I could see his nose sniffing ninety odors a minute and his mind racing. *Could it be? Could it really be? All this time, could Mom have been hiding the world's largest, most spectacular, most deliciously smelly rubber band?*

When we started pulling the Christmas tree out of the box, I could almost see Dewey's jaw drop.

It's not a rubber band, it's . . . it's . . . better.

As we pulled out each branch, Dewey lunged at it. He wanted to sniff and chew and steal every green piece of plastic sticking out of every green wire branch.

60

"Give me that, Dewey!" I yelled.

He coughed a few plastic tree needles onto the floor. Then he leaped into the box just as Cynthia was pulling out the next branch.

"Back off, Dewey."

Cynthia pulled him out, but a second later he was back, a green needle stuck to the moist tip of his nose. This time, his whole head disappeared inside the box.

"This isn't going to work, Dewey. Do you want me to get the rest of the tree out or not?"

Apparently the answer was not, because Dewey wasn't moving.

"All right, Dewey, out, out, out," Cynthia said, pulling on his behind. "I'd hate for you to lose an eye." Dewey got the message and jumped back, only to start burrowing under the pile of branches on the floor.

"This is going to take all day," Cynthia said.

"I sure hope so," I replied.

As Cynthia pulled the last branches out of the box, I started to assemble the tree. Dewey was prancing and grinning, watching my every move. He came in for a sniff and a taste, then bounced back a few feet. The poor cat looked like he was about to explode with excitement.

Hurry up, hurry up. I want my turn. This was the happiest I'd seen him all year.

"Oh, no, Dewey, not again."

Oh boy, Dewey had buried himself in the Christmas tree box again. This time, he disappeared completely inside, and a few seconds later the box was rolling back and forth across the floor. He stopped, poked his head out, and looked around. He spotted the half-assembled tree and bolted back to chew on the lower branches.

"I think he's found a new toy."

"I think he's found a new *love*," I said as I put the top branches into the notches on the trunk of our tree.

It was true. Dewey loved the Christmas tree. He loved the smell of it. The feel of it. The taste of it. Once I had it assembled and set up next to the circulation desk, he loved to sit under it. *Mine now*, he said as he rounded the base a few times. *Just leave us, thanks.*

"Sorry, Dewey. Still work to do. We don't even have it decorated yet."

Out came the ornaments: new tinsel, angels on strings, Santa Clauses, ribbons, bells, shiny balls with glitter all over them. One minute Dewey was crawling around in the boxes, finding out which ornaments came next. The next minute he was at our feet, playing with our shoelaces. Then he was stretching into the tree for another whiff of plastic. A few seconds later he was gone.

"What's that rustling sound?"

Suddenly Dewey came tearing by us with his head caught in one of the plastic grocery bags we used for storage. He ran all the way to the far side of the library, then came careening back toward us.

"Catch him!"

Dewey dodged and kept running, his head still caught in the bag. Soon he was on his way back. Cynthia blocked the area near the front door. I took the circulation desk. Dewey sprinted right between us. I could see from the look in his eyes he was in a frenzy. He had no idea how to get the plastic bag from around his neck. His only thought was, *Keep running. Maybe I can lose this monster.*

Soon there were four or five of us chasing him, but he wouldn't stop dodging and sprinting away. It didn't help that we were all laughing at him.

"Sorry, Dewey, but you've got to admit this is funny."

I finally cornered him and, despite his terrified squirming, managed to free him from the bag. Relieved, Dewey immediately went over to his new best friend, the Christmas tree, and lay down under the branches for a nice, comforting tongue bath. There would be a hair ball, no doubt, but at least a lesson had been learned: No plastic bags for the Dew.

The next step, now that the Christmas tree was up, was gifts. Every year, the librarians received a few gifts from grateful patrons. Eventually, they made a nice little stack of chocolates and cookies.

But our stack was dwarfed by Dewey's enormous pile of balls, treats, and toy mice. There were some fancy toys, even some nice homemade items, but Dewey's favorite new plaything wasn't a gift at all; it was some red yarn he found in a decorating box. That ball of yarn quickly became Dewey's constant companion.

He batted it around the library until a few feet of yarn stuck out, which he then pounced on, wrestled, and, very soon, got wrapped around his body. More than once, I was almost run down by an orange cat streaking across the library, red yarn around his legs and the bundle dragging behind him. An hour later, he'd be sacked out under the Christmas tree, all four feet clutching his big red buddy.

The library closed for three days on Christmas Eve, so Dewey came home with me. We spent Christmas morning together. I didn't give him a present, though. After a year together, our relationship was well beyond token gifts. We didn't have anything to prove.

All Dewey wanted from me was a few hours a day of my time. I felt the same way. So, that was what we gave each other—on our first Christmas and on every one that followed.

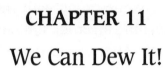

CHAPTER 11

We Can Dew It!

When I was growing up on a farm in Iowa, I thought the town of Moneta was big. It only had five hundred people, but it had a gas station, a dance hall, a restaurant, and a general store where kids would stand transfixed in front of a giant counter full of penny candies and whistles. There was a wonderful school and a baseball field. We even had bees. A local family had sixty hives and their honey was famous in four counties, which seemed like the whole wide world.

But do you know what happened to Moneta? It disappeared. Not closed down, I mean *gone,* like most of the buildings just got up and walked away. There's still a turnoff where the pavement turns into a dirt road, but there isn't a town. Not really. There are maybe ten houses, but there isn't a single open business. More than half the buildings on the old downtown strip from my childhood are gone, torn down to make way for a cornfield.

Even my farm is gone. We couldn't afford to keep it, so my dad sold it to our neighbor. That neighbor leveled our farmhouse, chopped down our trees, and turned the entire 160 acres into farmland. He even straightened our creek. I can drive by now without even recognizing it. The first four feet of our dirt driveway is all that remains of my childhood.

It's like that in Iowa. It's a great life, but it's also hard. Out here, there are rolling hills, but no mountains. There are rivers and creeks, but only a few lakes up in the county north of Spencer. The wind has worn down the rock outcroppings, turning them first to dust, then dirt, then soil. There's not much out here but fine black farm-land and long straight roads. And if something goes wrong, there aren't many ways to fix it. If the processing plant burns down, or the crops fail, or the bank goes under, your town could disappear. But we never thought that would happen to Spencer, even though times were tough.

I knew families were suffering. The parents never discussed their problems with me. They probably didn't discuss them with their closest friends. That's not the way they were; we didn't talk about our personal circumstances, be they good, bad, or indifferent. But you could tell.

One boy wore his old coat from the previous winter. His mother stopped wearing her makeup, then her jewelry. The boy loved Dewey; he clung to Dewey like a true friend, and his mother never stopped smiling when she saw them together. Then, around October, the boy and his mother stopped coming to the library. The family, I found out, had moved away.

And they weren't the only ones. In the late 1980s, the population of Spencer dropped from eleven thousand to eight thousand. People were leaving the county, even the state, looking for jobs. And there still weren't enough jobs in Spencer for the people that were left.

But we never lost faith. Do you know why? Because Spencer had been through worse. On June 27, 1931, at 1:36 p.m., an eight-year-old boy lit a sparkler outside Otto Bjornstad's drugstore at

Main and West Fourth Street. Someone screamed, and the startled boy dropped the sparkler into a large display of fireworks. The display exploded. The fire, whipped by a hot wind, spread across the street. Within minutes the blaze was burning down both sides of Grand Avenue. At the height of the blaze, even the pavement caught fire. By the end of the day, thirty-six buildings housing seventy-two businesses, more than half the businesses in town, were destroyed.

Can you imagine what those people thought as they looked at the smoke floating out over the fields and the smoldering remains of their beloved town? That afternoon northwest Iowa must have felt like a lonely place.

But do you know what they did? They started working. Within two days, the businesses were opening in barns and garages. Within a year, most of the buildings on Grand Avenue had been rebuilt bigger and better than ever. Around here, we call that progressive. If something bad happens, you don't complain about it, you use the opportunity to make it better. That's progressive.

And that's what happened during those bad times in the 1980s, back when the stores started closing and Christmas almost had to be canceled.

Instead of complaining, we became "progressive." We started working harder. We built parks; we fixed the sidewalk and streetlights downtown. We rebuilt the best hotel in town, which had fallen into ruin. Guess what we called it? You guessed it, the Hotel.

As library director, I wanted to do my part. My plan was to remodel the library. I knew the library wasn't just a place to keep books; it was a social center of town. A nice library would make everyone feel better. So as soon as I became library director, I started pressing for money to remodel. The city council made all the decisions, so that's where I went...again and again and again.

"Money for the library?" They laughed. "But we already have enough books."

"The library isn't a warehouse," I told them. "It's a community center. We have meeting rooms, story hours, computers. Newly paved roads are nice, but they don't lift our community's spirits. Not like a warm, friendly library. Wouldn't it be great to have a library we're proud of?"

"I got to be honest," they said. "I don't see how prettier books make a difference."

Then a funny thing happened: Dewey changed

everything. I wanted the library to feel more comfortable. Dewey made it feel like a home. I wanted people to come and spend more time at the library. Once Dewey arrived, more people started coming. And they were staying longer, too. They were leaving happier, and that happiness was being carried to their homes, their schools, and their jobs. Even better, people were talking.

"I was down at the library," someone would comment.

"Was Dewey there?"

"Of course."

"Did he sit in your lap? He always sits on my daughter's lap."

"Actually, I was reaching for a book on a high shelf, and instead of a book I accidently grabbed Dewey. I was so startled I dropped a book right on my toe."

"What did Dewey do?"

"He laughed."

"Really?"

"No, but I sure did."

It wasn't a remodel that changed the library; it was a cat! A wonderful, friendly, personable cat who made everyone welcome. That was Dewey's charm: he didn't play favorites. He loved everybody. And everybody loved him in return.

Eventually, even the city council started to notice the change. Slowly, their attitude shifted. They began to realize, thanks to Dewey, that the library was a social center for the town. And they discovered that a good library really could make people happy and proud.

And do you know what? After years of saying no, they finally said yes to the library remodel. And it was all because of Dewey.

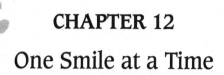

CHAPTER 12

One Smile at a Time

How did Dewey change the library? By changing the people who visited it, of course!

For instance, every week the library hosted a Story Hour for local special education classes. Before Dewey, the kids were poorly behaved. This was their big outing for the week and they were excited: screaming, yelling, jumping up and down. But Dewey changed that. As they got to know him, the children learned that if they were too noisy or erratic, Dewey left. They would do anything to keep Dewey with them; after a few months, they became so calm you couldn't believe it was the same group of kids.

Most of the children were physically limited, so they couldn't pet Dewey very well. Dewey didn't care. As long as the children were quiet, he spent the hour with them. He walked around the room and rubbed their legs. He jumped in their laps. The children became so fixated on him, they didn't notice anything else. If we had read them the phone book they wouldn't have cared.

Crystal was one of the more challenged members of the group. She was a beautiful girl of about eleven, but she had no speech and very little control of her limbs. She was in a wheelchair, and the wheelchair had a wooden tray on the front. When she came into the library, her head was always down and her eyes were staring at that tray. When the teacher took off her coat, she didn't even move. It was like she wasn't there.

Dewey noticed Crystal right away, but they didn't form an immediate bond. She didn't seem interested in him, and there were plenty of children who desperately wanted his attention. Then one week Dewey jumped on Crystal's wheelchair tray. Crystal squealed. She had been coming to the library for years, and I didn't even know she could make noises. That squeal was the first sound I ever heard her make.

After that, Dewey started visiting Crystal every week. Every time he jumped onto her tray, Crystal squealed with delight. It was a loud, high-pitched squeal, but it never scared Dewey. He knew what it meant. He could feel her excitement. Or maybe he could see the change in her face. Whenever she saw Dewey, Crystal glowed. Her eyes had always been blank. Now they were on fire.

Soon it wasn't just seeing Dewey on her tray that got Crystal excited. The moment the teacher pushed her into the library, Crystal was alive. When she saw Dewey, who usually waited for her at the front door, she immediately started to vocalize. It wasn't her usual high-pitched squeal but a deeper sound. I think she was calling to Dewey. Dewey must have thought so, too, because as soon as he heard it, he was at her side. Once her wheelchair was parked, he jumped on her tray, and she was so, so happy. She started to squeal, and her smile, you couldn't believe how big and bright it was. Crystal had the best smile in the world.

Usually Crystal's teacher picked up her hand

and helped her pet Dewey. The feel of his fur on her skin always brought on a round of louder and more delighted squeals. I swear, one day she looked up and made eye contact with me. She was overcome with joy, and she wanted to share the moment with someone. Yes, this was the same girl who for years never lifted her eyes from the floor.

One week I picked Dewey off Crystal's tray and put him inside her coat, which she was wearing half unzipped. She didn't even squeal. She just stared down at him in awe. She was so happy. Dewey was so happy. He had a chest to lean on, and it was warm, and he was with somebody he loved. He wouldn't come out of her coat. He stayed in there for twenty minutes. The other children checked out books. Dewey and Crystal sat together in front of the circulation desk. The bus was idling in front of the library, and all the other children were on it, but Dewey and Crystal were still sitting where we had left them, alone together. That moment was worth the world.

I can't imagine Crystal's life. I don't know how she felt when she was out in the world, or even what she did. But I know that whenever she was in the Spencer Public Library with Dewey, she was happy. And I think she experienced the kind of complete happiness very few of us ever feel. Dewey knew that. He wanted her to experience that happiness, and he loved her for it.

Isn't that a legacy worthy of any cat—or human being?

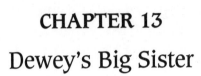

CHAPTER 13

Dewey's Big Sister

There was another special person Dewey helped as well. Have you guessed who it was? That's right: it was me.

I had a great life, I really did, but I'd also had some hard times. I didn't get to go to college; I had to work in a factory. I had health problems. I got divorced at age thirty—and I didn't even know how to drive a car! But maybe the hardest thing of all, if you can believe it, was seeing my daughter Jodi growing up.

When she was young, Jodi was my best friend. We walked our cockapoo, Brandy, together. We went window-shopping at the mall (because we couldn't afford to actually buy anything). We had sleepovers in the living room. *The Wizard of Oz*—over the rainbow where everything is in color and you have the power to do what you've always wanted if only you knew how to tap into it—came on television once a year. There were no video rental stores or DVDs or pay-per-view movies back then, so that was our only chance to see our favorite movie for the year. The night it came on, we would have a picnic and slee-pover in front of the television and talk and talk and talk about it all night long.

Even the two-hour drive to my parents' house in Hartley, Iowa, was fun. Jodi and I would laugh and sing along to corny seventies songs by John Denver and Barry Manilow. And we always played a special game. I would say, "Who's the biggest man you know?"

Jodi would answer, and then ask me, "Who's the strongest woman you know?"

I would answer and ask, "Who's the funniest woman you know?"

We asked questions back and forth until even-tually I could think of only one more question. "Who's the smartest woman you know?"

Jodi always answered, "You, Mommy." She had no idea how much I looked forward to hear-ing that.

Then Jodi turned ten. At ten, Jodi stopped answering the question.

At thirteen, we had moved to Spencer. After that, she stopped letting me kiss her good night. "I'm too old for that, Mommy," she said one night.

"I know," I told her. "You're a big girl now." But it broke my heart.

By the time Jodi was sixteen, I felt we were living separate lives. It wasn't her fault; a lot of times, that just happens.

And then came Dewey.

With Dewey, I had something to talk about that Jodi wanted to hear. I'd tell her what he did and who came to see him. The librarians alternated feeding Dewey on Sunday mornings when the library was closed. Although I was never able to get Jodi out of bed for those Sunday morning visits, we'd often drop by the library Sunday night on our way back from dinner at my parents' house.

You wouldn't believe Dewey's excitement when Jodi walked in that library door. The cat pranced. He would do backflips off bookshelves just to impress her.

Dewey never followed anyone around...

except Jodi. He was absolutely crazy about Jodi. Even when Jodi came to the library during work hours, Dewey sprinted to her side. He didn't care who saw him; he had no pride around that girl. As soon as she sat down, Dewey was in her lap.

I always brought Dewey home with me on holidays, when the library was closed for a few days. He spent the first couple of minutes crouched on the floor in the backseat—he always worried we were going to see his veterinarian Dr. Esterly—but as soon as he felt me turn onto Eleventh Street, he bounced up to stare out the window. As soon as I opened the door, he rushed into my house to give everything a nice long sniff. Then he ran up and down the basement stairs about a hundred times. He couldn't get enough of those stairs.

When he finally got tired, Dewey would often settle in beside me on the sofa. Just as often, though, he sat on the back of the sofa and stared out the window. He was watching for Jodi. When she came home, he jumped right up and ran to the door. As soon as she walked in, Dewey was Velcro.

He never left Jodi's side. He ran between her legs and almost tripped her. When she took her shower, he sat in the bathroom and stared at the shower curtain. If she closed the door, he sat right outside. If the shower stopped and she didn't come out quickly enough, he cried. As soon as she sat down, he was on her lap. It didn't matter if she was at the dinner table or on the toilet. He jumped on her, kneaded her stomach, and purred, purred, purred.

Jodi's room was an absolute mess. When it came to her appearance, my daughter was immaculate. Not a hair out of place. Put it this way: she ironed her socks. So who would believe her room looked like the lair of a troll? You couldn't see the floor, crusty plates and glasses were buried under dirty clothes, and the closet was so stuffed with junk you couldn't close the door. I refused to clean up after her, but I also refused to stop nagging her about it. Just like a typical mother, right?

But Dewey didn't care. Dirty room? Nagging mother? *That's Jodi in there,* he said to me with one last look as he disappeared behind her door for the night. *What does that other stuff matter?*

Sometimes, just before turning in for the night, Jodi would call me to her room. I'd walk in and find Dewey guarding Jodi's pillow. Other times, he'd be lying right on top of her face.

"Mmmm," she'd say as he rolled over onto her mouth. "Ah camf breeff."

I'd look at him for a second and then, suddenly...Jodi and I would both start laughing.

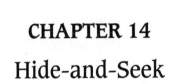

CHAPTER 14

Hide-and-Seek

Have you ever been in a library after closing? Of course not! (Or at least I hope not.) Well, let me tell you: a library after closing is a lonely place. It is very quiet, and the rows of shelves create a lot of dark and creepy corners. Most of the librarians I know won't stay alone in a library after dark. But I worked at the Spencer Public Library almost every night after everyone else had gone home, and I was never scared. I was strong. I was stubborn. And most of all, I was never alone. I had Dewey.

While I worked, Dewey sat on top of my computer screen, lazily swiping his tail back and forth. Type, swipe. Type, swipe. When I stopped, he always jumped down onto the keyboard. *No more,* he'd say. *Let's play.* Dewey had an amazing sense of timing.

"All right, Dewey," I told him. "You go first."

Dewey's game was hide-and-seek, so as soon as I gave the word he would take off around the corner. Half the time I spotted the back half of a long-haired orange cat immediately. To Dewey, hiding meant sticking your head into a bookshelf; he seemed to forget he had a tail.

"I wonder where Dewey is," I said out loud as I snuck up on him. "Boo!" I yelled when I got within a few feet, sending Dewey running.

Other times he was better hidden. I would sneak around a few shelves with no luck, then turn the corner to see him prancing toward me with that big Dewey smile.

You couldn't find me! You couldn't find me!

"That's not fair, Dewey. You only gave me twenty seconds."

Occasionally he curled up in a tight spot and stayed put. I'd look for five minutes, then start calling his name. "Dewey! Dewey!" That dark library could get a little scary, but I always imagined Dewey hiding just a few feet away, laughing at me.

"All right, Dewey, that's enough. You win!"

Nothing. Where could that cat be? Just when I was giving up, I'd turn around and there he was, standing in the middle of the aisle, staring at me.

"Oh, Dewey, you clever boy. Now it's my turn."

I'd run and hide behind a bookshelf, and invariably one of two things happened. I'd get to my hiding place, turn around, and Dewey would be standing right there. He had followed me.

Found you. That was easy.

His other favorite thing to do was run around the other side of the shelf and beat me to my hiding spot.

Oh, is this where you're thinking about hiding? Because, well, I've already figured it out.

I'd laugh and pet him behind the ears. "Fine, Dewey. Let's just run for a while."

We'd run between the shelves, meeting at the end of the aisles, nobody quite hiding and no one really seeking. After fifteen minutes I would completely forget my troubles. Whatever had been bothering me, it was gone. The weight, as they say, was lifted.

"Okay, Dewey. Let's get back to work."

Dewey never complained. I'd climb back into my chair, and he'd climb back on top of the computer and start waving his tail in front of the screen. The next time I needed him, he'd be there.

It's not a stretch to say those games of hide-and-seek with Dewey got me through a lot of hard nights. Maybe I should tell you Dewey put his head on my lap and whimpered while I cried, or that he licked the tears from my face. You could understand that, right? And it is almost true, because sometimes when the ceiling started falling in on me and I found myself staring blankly down at my lap, tears in my eyes, Dewey was there, right where I needed him to be.

Dewey was a loving cat—he was always a soft touch, for instance, for a late-night cuddle. But he was still a cat, so he liked his personal space. He didn't just bathe me with affection all the time. Somehow, though, he always knew when I needed a little nudge or a warm body, and he knew when the best thing for me was a silly, mindless game of hide-and-seek.

And whatever I needed, he'd give me, without thought, without wanting something in return, and without me asking. It wasn't just love. It was more than that. It was respect. It was empathy. And it went both ways. That connection Dewey and I had felt when we met? Those nights alone together in the library turned it into an unbreakable bond.

CHAPTER 15

The Dewkster

We started remodeling the Spencer Public Library in the spring, just as northwest Iowa was waking up and changing from brown to green. The lawns suddenly needed mowing, and the trees on Grand Avenue were throwing out new leaves. On the farms, the plants were pushing through the soil, and you could finally see the result of all that time spent fixing equipment, churning fields, and planting seeds. The weather turned warm. The kids brought out bicycles. At the library, after a year of planning, it was finally time to get to work.

The first step was painting the bare concrete walls. Tony Joy, our painter and the husband of staff member Sharon Joy, threw some drop cloths over the books and leaned his ladder against the shelves. Easy, right? But as soon as his ladder went in, Dewey climbed up.

"All right, Dewey," Tony said. "Down you go."

Dewey wasn't paying attention. He'd been in the library more than a year, but he'd never seen it from nine feet up. With a few steps along the top of the bookshelves, he was out of reach.

Tony moved the ladder. Dewey moved again. Tony climbed to the top of the ladder, propped his elbow on the bookshelf, and looked at this stubborn cat.

"This is a bad idea, Dewey. I'm going to paint this wall, then you're going to rub against it. Vicki's going to see a blue cat, and then you know what's going to happen? I'm going to get fired."

Dewey just stared.

"You don't care, do you?"

I wasn't worried about Dewey. He was the most conscientious cat I'd ever known. He raced down bookshelves without a misstep. He intentionally brushed displays with his side, but never knocked them over. I knew he could not only walk on a shelf without touching wet paint, but also tiptoe up a ladder without knocking off the paint can at the top. I was more worried about Tony. It's not easy sharing a ladder with the King of the Library.

"I'll take my chances," Tony joked. "As long as you don't blame me for the big blue cat."

Within a few days, Tony and Dewey were fast friends. Or maybe I should say Tony and Dewkster, because that's what Tony always called him: The Dewkster. Tony felt Dewey was too soft a name for such a macho cat. He worried the local alley cats were assembling outside the library window at night to make fun of his name. So Tony decided his real name wasn't Dewey, it was the Duke. "Only his close friends call him Dewkster," Tony explained.

When Tony finished the painting three weeks later, Dewey was a changed cat. Maybe he thought he really was the Duke, because suddenly he wasn't content with just naps and laps. He wanted to explore. And climb. And most important, explore new places to climb. We called this Dewey's Edmund Hillary phase, after the famous mountain climber. (Sir Edmund Hillary was the first Westerner to climb Mount Everest.) Dewey didn't want to stop climbing until he'd reached the top of his personal Mount Everest, which he managed to do about a month later.

"Any sign of Dewey this morning?" I asked Audrey Wheeler, who was working at the circulation desk. "He didn't come for breakfast."

"I haven't seen him."

"Let me know if you do. I want to make sure he's not sick."

Five minutes later I heard Audrey utter what around here was a surprising profanity: "Oh, my golly!"

She was standing in the middle of the library, looking straight up. And there, on top of the ceiling lights, looking straight down, was Dewey.

When he saw us looking, Dewey pulled his head back. He was instantly invisible. As we watched, Dewey's head reappeared a few feet down the light. Then it disappeared again. Then it appeared a few feet farther on. Dewey had figured out how to climb up on top of the lights. He had clearly been up there for hours, watching us.

"How are we going to get him down?"

"Maybe we should call the city," someone suggested. "They'll send someone with a ladder."

"Let's just wait him out," I said. "He's not doing any harm up there, and he'll have to come down for food eventually."

An hour later Dewey trotted into my office, licking his lips from a late breakfast, and jumped into my lap. He was clearly keyed up about this new game, but didn't want to overplay his hand. I knew he was dying to ask, *What do you think of that?*

"I'm not even going to mention it, Dewey."

He cocked his head at me.

"I'm serious."

Okay then, I'll nap. Exciting morning, you know.

It took a few weeks for us to figure out his method of getting up to the lights. It was pretty ingenious. First, Dewey jumped on an empty computer desk. Then he jumped on a filing cabinet. That gave him a long jump to the top of the temporary wall around the staff area, where he could hide behind a huge quilt of Spencer history. From there, it was only four feet to the lights.

Sure, we could have rearranged the furniture, but once he figured it all out we knew there wasn't much, except old age and creaky bones, that could stop Dewey from walking the lights. When cats don't know something exists, it's easy to keep them away. If they can't get to something they've made up their minds they want, it's almost impossible. Cats aren't lazy; they'll put in the work to thwart even the best-laid plans.

Besides, Dewey loved being up on the lights. He loved walking back and forth from end to end until he found an interesting spot. Then he would lie down, drape his head over the side, and watch. The patrons loved it, too. Sometimes when Dewey was pacing you could see them craning up at the ceiling, their heads going back and forth like clock pendulums. When Dewey was pointed out to the children, his head just peeking over the edge of the lights, they screamed with excitement. They had so many questions.

"What's he doing?"

"How'd he get up there?"

"Why is he up there?"

"Will he get burned?"

"What if he falls off? Will he die?"

"What if he falls on somebody? Will they die?"

When the children found out they couldn't join him on the ceiling, they begged him to come down. "Dewey likes it up there," we explained. "He's playing." Eventually even the children understood that when Dewey was on the lights, he was coming down only on his terms. He had discovered his own little heaven up there.

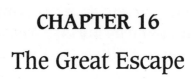

CHAPTER 16

The Great Escape

By August, the remodeling was over. Attendance was up. The staff was happy. Dewey had not only been accepted by the town of Spencer, but people were inspired by him. The Clay County Fair, the biggest event of the year, was just around the corner in September. Everything was perfect—except Dewey. My contented baby boy, our library hero, was a changed cat: distracted, jumpy, and most of all, trouble.

During the remodel, big heavy things were constantly being moved in and out of the library, so Dewey had spent three weeks that summer at my house. Now, late summer is the best time of year in Spencer. The corn is ten feet high, golden and green. The sun is warm. The fields go on and on and on. You leave the windows open, just to catch the scent. It's hard, sometimes, to stay inside.

All day, Dewey stared through my window screens at the world outside. He couldn't see the corn, but he could hear the birds. He could feel the breeze. He could smell whatever cats smell when they direct their noses to the great outdoors.

Now he missed it. There were windows in the library, but they didn't open. You could smell the new carpet but not the outdoors. You could hear the trucks, but not the birds. *How can you show me something so wonderful,* he seemed to whine, *then take it away?*

At the front of the Spencer Public Library was a tiny lobby with glass doors on both sides. For two years Dewey hated that lobby; when he returned from his three weeks at my house, he adored it. From the lobby, he could hear the birds. When the outer doors were open, he could smell fresh air. For a few hours in the afternoon, there was even a patch of sunlight. Dewey loved sunlight! He pretended that was all he wanted, to sit in that patch of sun and listen to the birds.

But we knew better. Dewey really wanted to go through that second set of doors and into the outside world.

"Dewey, get back in here!" a librarian would yell every time he followed a patron into the lobby. The circulation desk faced the lobby; the poor cat had no chance of not being seen. So Dewey stopped listening.

Eventually, the library staff started coming back to get me. I was Mom. Dewey always listened to me. Or at least he used to. Now I had to resort to more serious methods.

"Dewey, do you want me to get the bottle?" I'd say when he refused to come out of the lobby.

He'd just stared at me.

I'd bring the squirt bottle, which Dewey hated as much as his baths, out from behind my back. With the other arm, I'd hold open the door to the library. Dewey would slink back inside.

Ten minutes later: "Vicki, Dewey's in the lobby again!"

Finally, I'd had enough. No more Mrs. Nice Mom. I stormed out of my office, used my best Mom voice, threw open the lobby door, and demanded, "You get in here right now, young man."

Unfortunately, a real young man was sitting in the lobby, and he almost jumped out of his skin when the crazy lady started yelling. Before the last word was out of my mouth, he had rushed into the library, grabbed a magazine, and buried his head in it all the way up to the fine print. Talk about embarrassing. I was holding the door open in stunned silence, unable to believe I hadn't seen this guy right in front of my face, when Dewey came trotting past like nothing had happened. I could almost see him smiling.

A week later, I couldn't find Dewey anywhere. Nothing unusual there; Dewey had plenty of places to hide. There was a cubbyhole behind the display case by the front door that was about the size of a box of crayons. There was the brown lounge chair in the children's area, although his tail usually stuck out of that one. Then there was "between the books." In a library, books fit on both sides of a shelf. Between the two rows is about four inches of space. "Between the books" was Dewey's ultimate hiding place. The only way to find him was to lift books and look behind them. That doesn't sound so difficult until you consider that the Spencer Public Library contained more than four hundred shelves of books. Between those books was an enormous labyrinth, a long, narrow world all Dewey's own.

Fortunately he almost always stuck to his favorite place: the bottom row of Westerns. Not this time. He wasn't under the brown lounger, either, or in his cubbyhole. I didn't notice him peeking down from the lights. I opened the doors to the bathrooms to see if he had been locked inside. Not this morning.

"Has anyone seen Dewey?"

No. No. No. No.

"Who locked up last night?"

"I did," Joy said, "and he was definitely here." I knew Joy would never have forgotten to look for Dewey. She was the only librarian, besides me, who would stay late with him to play hide-and-seek.

"Good. He must be in the building. Looks like he's found a new hiding place."

But when I returned from lunch, Dewey was still missing. And he hadn't touched his food. That's when I began to worry.

"Where's Dewey?" a patron asked.

We had already heard that question twenty times. I told the staff, "Tell them Dewey's not feeling well. No need to alarm anyone." He'd show up. I knew it.

That night, I drove around for half an hour instead of heading straight home. I wasn't expecting to see a fluffy orange cat prowling the neighborhood, but you never know. The thought going through my mind was, *What if he's hurt? What if he needs me, and I can't find him? I'm letting him down.* I knew he hadn't run away. But...

He wasn't waiting for me at the front door the next day. I stepped inside and the place felt dead. A cold dread walked up my spine, even though it was ninety degrees outside. I knew something was wrong.

I told the staff, "Look everywhere."

We checked every corner. We opened every cabinet and drawer. We pulled books off the shelves, hoping to find him in his crawl space. We shined a flashlight behind the wall shelves. Some of them had pulled an inch or two away from the wall; Dewey could have been making his rounds, fallen in, and gotten stuck. Clumsiness wasn't like him, but in an emergency you check every possibility.

The night janitor! The thought hit me like

a rock, and I picked up the phone. "Hi, Virgil, it's Vicki at the library. Did you see Dewey last night?"

"Who?"

"Dewey. The cat."

"Nope. Didn't see him."

"Is there anything he could have gotten into that made him sick? Cleaning solution maybe?"

He hesitated. "Don't think so."

I didn't want to ask, but I had to. "Do you ever leave any doors open?"

He really hesitated this time. "I prop open the back door when I take out the garbage."

"How long?"

"Maybe five minutes."

"Did you prop it open two nights ago?"

"I prop it open every night."

My heart sank. That was it. Dewey would never just run out an open door, but if he had a week to think about it, peek around the corner, sniff the air . . .

"Do you think he ran out?" Virgil asked.

"Yes, Virgil, I do."

We set up shifts so that two people could cover the library while the rest of us looked for Dewey. The regular patrons could tell something was wrong. "Where's Dewey?" went from an innocent inquiry to an expression of concern. We continued to tell most patrons nothing was wrong, but we took the regulars aside and told them Dewey was missing. Soon a dozen people were walking the sidewalks. *Look at all these people. Look at all this love. We'll find him now,* I told myself again and again.

I was wrong.

I spent my lunch hour walking the streets, looking for my baby boy. He was so sheltered in the library. He wasn't a fighter. He was a finicky eater. How was he going to survive?

On the kindness of strangers, I thought. Dewey trusted people. He wouldn't hesitate to ask for help.

I dropped in on Mr. Fonley at Fonley Flowers, which had a back entrance off the alley behind the library. He hadn't seen Dewey. Neither had Rick Krebsbach at the photo studio. I called all the veterinarians in town. We didn't have an animal shelter, so a vet's office was the place someone would take him. I told the vets, "If someone brings in a cat who looks like Dewey, it probably is Dewey. We think he's escaped."

I told myself, *Everyone knows Dewey. Everyone*

loves Dewey. If someone finds him, they'll bring
him back to the library.

I didn't want to spread the news that he was missing. Dewey had so many children who loved him, not to mention the special needs students. Oh, my goodness, what about his friend Crystal? I didn't want to scare them. I knew Dewey was coming back.

When Dewey wasn't waiting for me at the front door on the third morning, my stomach plummeted. I realized that, in my heart, I had been expecting to see him sitting there. When he wasn't, I was devastated. That's when it hit me: Dewey was gone. He probably wasn't coming back. I knew Dewey was important, but only at that moment did I realize how big a hole he would leave. To the town of Spencer, Dewey *was* the library. How could we go on without him? How could I go on without him?

The mood in the library was black. Yesterday we had hope. We believed it was only a matter of time. Now we believed he was gone. We continued to search, but we had looked everywhere. I sat down and thought about what I was going to tell the community. I would call the radio station. They would immediately make an announcement. They could mention an orange cat without saying his name. The adults would understand; maybe they could keep it from the children for a while.

"Vicki!"

Then the newspaper. They would run the story tomorrow. Maybe someone had taken him in.

"Vicki!"

Should we put up flyers? What about a reward?

"Vicki!"

Who was I kidding? He was gone. If he was here, we would have found—

"Vicki! Guess who's home!"

I stuck my head out of the office and there he was, my big orange buddy, wrapped in the arms of Jean Hollis Clark. I rushed over and hugged him. He laid his head on my chest.

"Oh, baby boy, baby boy. Don't ever do that again."

Dewey didn't need me to tell him. I could tell this was no joke. Dewey was purring like he had on our first morning. He was so happy to see me, so thankful to be in my arms. But I knew him so well. Underneath, in his bones, he was still shaking.

"I found him under a car on Grand Avenue," Jean was saying. "I was going over to White Drug, and I happened to catch a glimpse of orange out of the corner of my eye."

I wasn't listening. I would hear the story many times over the next few days, but at that moment I wasn't listening. I only had eyes and ears for Dewey.

"He was hunched against the wheel under a car. I called to him, but he didn't come. He looked like he wanted to run, but he was too afraid. He must have been right there all along. Can you believe that? All those people looking for him, and he was right there all along."

The rest of the staff was crowding around us now. I could tell they wanted to cuddle him, but I didn't want to let him go.

"He needs to eat," I told them. Someone put out a fresh can of food, and we all watched while Dewey sucked it down. I doubt he had eaten in days.

Once he had done his business—food, water, litter box—I let the staff hold him. He was passed from hand to hand like a hero in a victory parade. When everyone had welcomed him home, we took him out to show the public. Most of them didn't know anything had happened, but there were a few wet eyes.

That afternoon I gave Dewey a bath, which he tolerated for the first time since that cold January morning so long ago. He was covered in motor oil, which took months to work out of his long fur. He had a tear in one ear and a scratch on his nose. I cleaned them gently.

Was it another cat? A loose wire? The under-carriage of a car? I rubbed his cut ear between my fingers, and Dewey didn't even flinch. "What happened out there?" I wanted to ask him, but the two of us had already come to an under-standing. We would never talk about this inci-dent again.

Years later, I would make it a habit to prop open a door during library board meetings. Cathy Greiner, a board member, asked me every time, "Aren't you worried Dewey will run out?"

I looked down at Dewey, who was always there to attend the meeting. He looked up at me. That look told me, as clearly as if he'd crossed his heart and hoped to die, that he wasn't going to run. Why couldn't everyone else see it?

"He's not going anywhere," I told her. "He's committed to the library."

And he was. For sixteen years, Dewey never went into the lobby again. He lounged by the door, especially in the morning, but he never followed patrons out. If the doors opened and he heard trucks, he sprinted to the staff area. He didn't want to be anywhere near a passing truck. Dewey was completely done with the outdoors. He was really and truly a library cat.

THE DAILY ROUTINE

As developed by Dewey Readmore Books soon after his regrettable romp outside the Spencer Public Library, and followed for the rest of his life.

7:30 A.M.

Mom arrives. Demand food, but don't be too hasty. Watch everything she does. Follow at her heels. Make her feel special.

8:00 A.M.

Staff arrives. Spend an hour checking in with everyone. Find out who is having a tough morning and give her the honor of petting me for as long as she wants. Or until ...

8:58 A.M.

Prep time. Take up position by the front door, ready for first patron of the day. This also has the added benefit of alerting distracted staff of current time. I hate it when they open late.

9:00–10:30 A.M.

Doors open. Greet patrons. Follow the nice ones, but give everyone a chance to brighten their day by paying attention to me. Petting me is a gift for visiting the library.

10:30 A.M.

Find lap for nap. Laps are for naps, not playing. Playing in laps is for kittens.

11:30–11:45 A.M.

Lounge. Middle of Adult Nonfiction, head up, paws crossed in front. The humans call this the Buddha pose. I call it the Lion King. *Hakuna matata.* No, I don't know what it means, but the kids keep talking about it.

11:45 A.M.–12:15 P.M.

Sprawl. When it gets too tiring to hold head up, assume the sprawl: full out on back, paws sticking out in four directions. Petting is assured. But don't fall asleep. Fall asleep, and you're vulnerable to a belly wrestle attack. I hate belly wrestle attacks.

12:15–12:30 P.M.

Lunch in the staff room. Anybody got yogurt? No? Then never mind.

12:30–1:00 P.M.

Cart ride! When the clerks shelve books, jump on the cart and hitch a ride around the library. Oh, man, it's relaxing to go completely limp and let my legs hang down between the bars of the metal rack.

1:00–3:45 P.M.

Afternoon free time. See how the day is going. Mix in a trip up to the lights with more lap time. Greet the afternoon crowd. Spend ten minutes with Mom. Fur licking is encouraged, not mandatory. And don't forget to find a nice box to nap in. As if it's possible to forget that!

3:55 P.M.

Dinner. They keep thinking dinnertime is four o'clock. If I sit here long enough, they'll learn.

5:05 P.M.

Mom leaves. Jump around so she'll remember I want to play. A running jump off a bookshelf, complete with somersault, works every time.

5:30 P.M.

Play. Mom calls it Boodha Track because that's what the letters on the side say. I guess that's the "real name." I call it the Ball Thingy because there's nothing better than batting that ball around that track. Except for playing with my red yarn. I absolutely love my red yarn. Does anyone want to dangle it for me?

9:05 P.M.

Last shift leaves. Repeat 5:05 routine, but don't expect the same results unless Joy's working the night shift. Joy always finds time to wad up paper and toss it across the library. Sprint after the paper as fast as possible, but once I get there, always ignore it.

9:10 P.M.–7:30 A.M.

My time! None of your business, nosy!

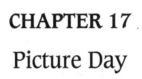

CHAPTER 17

Picture Day

About two months after Dewey's escape, I took him for his first official photograph. I'd like to say it was for sentimental reasons, or that I realized Dewey was on the cusp of something far bigger than either of us ever imagined, but the real reason was a coupon. Rick Krebsbach, the town photographer, was offering pet photographs for ten dollars.

Dewey was such an easygoing cat that I convinced myself that having a professional portrait taken, in a professional portrait studio, would be easy. But Dewey hated the studio. As soon as we walked in, his head was swiveling around, his eyes staring at everything. I put him in the chair, and he immediately hopped out. I picked him up and put him in the chair again. I took one step back, and Dewey was gone.

"He's nervous," I said as I watched Dewey sniff the photo backdrop. "He hasn't been out of the library much."

"That's nothing," Rick said as we watched Dewey dig his head under a pillow. "One dog tried to bite my camera. Another dog actually ate my fake flowers. Now that I think about it, he puked on that pillow."

I quickly picked up Dewey. He was still looking around, more nervous than interested.

"There's been quite a bit of, um…unfortunate peeing," Rick said. "I had to throw away a sheet. To an animal like Dewey, it must smell like a zoo."

"He's not used to other animals," I said. The truth, though, was that Dewey never cared about other animals. He always ignored the Seeing Eye dog who came into the library. He even ignored the Dalmatian that stared through the window at him almost every day. This wasn't fear; it was confusion.

"He knows what's expected of him in the library, but he doesn't understand this place."

"Take your time."

A thought. "May I show Dewey the camera?"

"If you think it will help."

Dewey posed for photographs at the library all the time, but those were personal cameras. Rick's camera was a large professional model. Dewey had never seen one of those before, but he was a fast learner.

"It's a camera, Dewey. Camera. We're here to get your picture taken."

Dewey sniffed the lens. He leaned back and looked at it, then sniffed it again.

I pointed. "Chair. Sit in the chair."

I put him down. He sniffed up and down every leg, and twice on the seat. Then he jumped into the chair and stared right at the camera. Rick hurried over and snapped six photos.

"I can't believe it," he said as Dewey climbed down off the chair.

I didn't want to tell Rick, but this happened all the time. Dewey always seemed to know what I wanted. Unfortunately that didn't mean he was always going to obey. I didn't even have to say *brush* or *bath*; all I had to do was *think* about them, and Dewey disappeared. I remember passing him in the library one afternoon. He looked up at me with his usual lazy indifference. *Hi, how you doing?*

I thought, *Oh, there are two knots of fur on his neck. I should get the scissors and cut them off.* As soon as the idea formed in my mind, *whoosh*, Dewey was gone.

But since his escape, Dewey had been using his powers for good, not mischief. He not only anticipated what I wanted, he did it. Not when a brushing or a bath was involved, of course, but for library business. That was one reason he was so willing to have his photograph taken. He wanted to do what was best for the library.

"He knows it's for the library," I told Rick, but I could tell he wasn't buying it. Why would a cat care about a library? And how could he connect a library with a photo studio a block away? But it was the truth, and I knew it.

I picked Dewey up and petted his favorite spot, the top of his head between the ears. "He knows what a camera is. He's not afraid of it."

"Has he ever posed before?"

"At least two or three times a week. For visitors. He loves it."

"That doesn't sound like a cat."

I wanted to tell him Dewey wasn't just any cat,

but Rick had been taking pet photographs all week. He'd probably heard it a hundred times already.

And yet if you see Dewey's official photograph, which Rick shot that day (it's on the cover of this book, so stop and look at it if you want), you can tell immediately he's not just another cat. He's beautiful, yes, but more than that, he's relaxed. He has no fear of the camera. His eyes are wide and clear. His fur is perfectly groomed. He doesn't look like a kitten, but he doesn't look like a grown cat, either. He's like a young man getting his high school graduation photograph taken: his posture is remarkably straight, his head cocked, his eyes staring calmly into the future. I smile every time I see that photo because he looks so serious. He looks like he's trying to be strong and handsome but can't quite pull it off because he's so darn cute.

A few days after receiving the finished photographs, I noticed the Spencer Shopko, a large general merchandise store sort of like Wal-Mart, was holding a pet photo contest to raise money for charity. You paid a dollar to vote, and the money was used to fight muscular dystrophy.

On a whim, I entered Dewey in the contest.

The photo was for library promotion, and wasn't this a perfect opportunity to promote this special aspect of the library? A few weeks later, Shopko strung a dozen photos, all of cats and dogs, on a wire in the front of the store. The town voted, and Dewey won by a landslide. He got more than 80 percent of the votes, seven times as many as the runner-up. It was ridiculous. When the store called to tell me the results, I was almost embarrassed.

Part of the reason Dewey won so overwhelmingly was the beautiful photograph.

Part of the reason was Dewey's looks. He's so handsome you'd have to love him.

Part of the reason was Dewey's personality. Most cats in photographs look scared to death, desperate to pee, disgusted by the whole process—or often all three. Most dogs look like they are about to go absolutely bonkers, knock over everything in the room, get themselves wound up in an electrical cord, and then eat the camera. Dewey looks calm.

But mostly, Dewey trounced the competition because the town had adopted him. Not just the regular library patrons, but the whole town. While I wasn't watching, Dewey had been quietly working his magic. The stories, not just about his rescue but about his life, were seeping down into the cracks and sprouting new life. He wasn't just the library's cat. He was Spencer's cat. He was our inspiration, our friend, our survivor. He was one of us. And at the same time, he belonged to us.

Was he a mascot for Spencer, the way he was for the library? No. But did he make a difference in the way the town thought about itself? Absolutely. Dewey reminded us, once again, that we were a different kind of place. We cared. We valued the small things.

Dewey was one more reason to love this hardy little town on the Iowa plains.

CHAPTER 18

Dewey Makes Headlines

It's amazing: sometimes when you stop running and start relaxing, the world comes to you. Or if not the world, then at least Iowa. Soon after the Shopko contest, Dewey was the subject of Chuck Offenburger's Iowa Boy column in the *Des Moines Register*. Iowa Boy was one of those columns that said things like, "It was the most shocking piece of news I'd come across since the time a few years ago I found out the Cleghorn Public Library, just down the road a ways, had started checking out cake pans to its patrons." Yes, in Iowa, many of the libraries have pans for baking cakes.

When I read the article about Dewey, I thought, *Wow, the Dew's really made it*. It was one thing

Nine weeks old on a giant dictionary—
I'm the definition of a-DEW-rable.

Don't worry. I'm too little to
knock the statue off the table.

Is it time for story hour yet?

That's right.
I'm after the clacker thingies again!

Caught red pawed!
I can tackle this yarn, I know I can.

You can have all the presents. I'll keep
my Christmas tree, thank you very much.

Take me to aisle D, please.
D for Dewey!

Look at my magnificent tail! I love it up here!

"Hello, and welcome to the library!"
See, I can easily work in my sleep.

What do you mean you're trying to work here?
I'm just trying to help.

It's fun to let your belly
hang out sometimes.

Peekaboo to you, too!
I need my nap right now!

I'll give you my back leg
if you promise . . . NO belly rub!

I know that I'm in the tax form box. You can
still reach under me for one. I don't mind.

I'm *way* cuter
than these other cats!

Thanks for the cuddle, Mom.
I love you, too!

for a town to adopt a cat. It was even better for a region to adopt that cat, as northwest Iowa had with Dewey. The library received visitors every day from small towns and farms in surrounding counties. Summer residents of the Iowa lake country drove down to meet him, then spread the word to their neighbors and guests, who would drive down the following week. He appeared frequently in the newspapers of nearby towns.

But the *Des Moines Register*! That was the daily newspaper in the state capital. The *Des Moines Register* was read all over the state. More than half a million people were probably reading about Dewey right now. That was more people than attend the Clay County Fair!

After Iowa Boy, Dewey started making regular appearances on our local television newscasts, which originated out of Sioux City, Iowa, and Sioux Falls, South Dakota. Soon he began appearing on stations in other cities and states. Every segment started the same way, with a voice-over: "The Spencer Library wasn't expecting anything more in their drop box than books on a freezing January morning..." No matter how they framed it, the picture was the same. A poor kitten, almost frozen to death, begging for help. The story of Dewey's arrival at the library was irresistible.

But so was his personality. Most news crews weren't used to filming cats—there were thousands of cats in northwest Iowa, no doubt, but few ever made it on television—so they always started out with what seemed like a good idea: "Just have him act natural."

"Well, there he is, sleeping in a box with his tail hanging out and his stomach oozing over the side. That's as natural as it gets."

Five seconds later: "Maybe he can jump or something?"

Dewey always gave them what they wanted. He jumped over the camera for a flying action shot. He walked between two displays to show his dexterity. He ran and jumped off the end of a shelf. He played with a child. He played with his red yarn. He sat quietly on top of the computer and stared into the camera. He wasn't showing off. Posing for the camera was part of Dewey's job as publicity director for the library, so he did it. Enthusiastically!

Dewey's appearance on *Living in Iowa*, an Iowa Public Television series that focuses on issues, events, and people in the state of Iowa, was typical. The *Living in Iowa* crew met me at the library at seven-thirty in the morning. Dewey was ready. He rolled. He jumped between the shelves. He walked up and put his nose on the camera. He stuck right by the side of the beautiful young host, totally winning her over.

"Can I hold him?" she asked.

I showed her the Dewey Carry—over the left shoulder (never the right!), with his behind in the crook of your arm. If you wanted to hold him for any length of time, you had to use the Dewey Carry.

"He's doing it!" the host whispered excitedly as Dewey draped over her shoulder.

Dewey's head popped up. *What did she say?*

"How do I get him to calm down?"

"Just pet him."

The host stroked his back. Dewey lay his head on her shoulder and cuddled against her neck. "He's doing it! He's really doing it! I can feel him purring."

I was tempted to tell her, "Of course he's doing it. He does it for everyone," but why spoil her excitement?

Dewey's episode aired a few months later. It was called "A Tale of Two Kitties." (It's a play on the famous Charles Dickens book *A Tale of Two Cities*.) The other kitty was Tom, who lived in Kibby's Hardware in Conrad, Iowa. Like Dewey, Tom was found on the coldest night of the year.

Store owner Ralph Kibby took the frozen stray to the vet's office. "They gave him sixty dollars' worth of shots," he said on the program, "and said if he's still alive in the morning he may have a chance." As I watched the show, I realized why the host was so happy with Dewey that morning. There were at least thirty seconds of footage of Dewey lying on her shoulder; the best she could get from Tom was a sniff of her finger.

Well, now Dewey was really famous. Pretty soon we had three or four people a week coming into the library to show Dewey off to their friends. "We're here to see the famous cat," an older man said, approaching the desk.

"He's sleeping in the back. I'll go get him."

"Thanks," he said, motioning to a younger woman with a little blond girl hiding behind her leg. "I wanted my granddaughter Lydia to meet him. She's from Kentucky."

When Lydia saw Dewey, she smiled and looked up at her grandfather. "Go ahead, sweetie. Dewey won't bite." The girl tentatively stretched out her hand to Dewey; two minutes later she was stretched out on the floor, petting him.

"See?" her grandfather said to the little girl's mother. "I told you it was worth the trip."

Later, while the mother was petting Dewey with her daughter, the grandfather came up to me and said, "Thanks so much for adopting Dewey." It seemed he wanted to say more, but I think we both understood he had already said enough. Thirty minutes later, as they were leaving, I heard the young woman tell the older man, "You were right, Dad. That was great. I wish we had come by sooner."

"Don't worry, Mommy," the little girl said. "We'll see Dewey next year, too."

BASIC RULES FOR CATS WHO HAVE A LIBRARY TO RUN

(ACCORDING TO DEWEY READMORE BOOKS)
FIRST PRINTED IN THE LIBRARY CAT SOCIETY NEWSLETTER,
AND SINCE REPRINTED NUMEROUS TIMES AROUND THE WORLD.

STAFF: If you are feeling particularly lonely and wanting more attention from the staff, sit on whatever papers, project, or computer they happen to be working on at the time—but sit with your back to the person and act aloof, so as not to appear too needy. Also, be sure to continually rub against the leg of the staff person who is wearing dark brown, blue, or black for maximum effect.

PATRONS: No matter how long the patron plans on staying at the library, climb into their briefcase or book bag for a long comfortable sleep until they must dump you out on the table in order to leave.

LADDERS: Never miss an opportunity to climb on ladders. It does not matter which human is on the ladder. It only matters that you get to the top and stay there.

CLOSING TIME: Wait until ten minutes before closing time to get up from your nap. Just as the staff is getting ready to turn out the lights and lock the door, do all your cutest tricks in an effort to get them to stay and play with you. (Although this doesn't work very often, sometimes they can't resist giving in to one short game of hide-and-seek.)

5 **BOXES:** Your humans must realize that all boxes that enter the library are yours. It doesn't matter how large, how small, or how full the box should be, it is yours! If you cannot fit your entire body into the box, then use whatever part of your body fits to assume ownership for nap time. (I have used one or two paws, my head, or even just my tail to gain entry, and each works equally well for a truly restful sleep.)

6 **MEETINGS:** No matter the group, timing, or subject matter, if there is a meeting scheduled in the meeting room, you have an obligation to attend. If they have shut you out by closing the door, cry pitifully until they let you in or until someone opens the door to use the restroom or get a drink of water. After you gain entry, be sure to go around the room and greet each attendee. If there is a film or slide show, climb on any table close to the screen, settle in, and watch the film to its conclusion. As the credits roll, feign extreme boredom and leave the meeting before it ends.

And the library cat's golden rule for all time . . .

Never forget, nor let humans forget, that you own the joint!

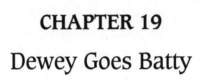

CHAPTER 19

Dewey Goes Batty

When Dewey was six, the Spencer Public Library received a technology update. Out went the catalog cards—you've never even heard of those, have you? I admit, they are pretty old-fashioned—and in came the computers. Now, some people think computers are cold, meaning they make you stare at a screen instead of talking to a person. Dewey disagreed. Dewey thought they were warm. Literally. He loved to sit on them and bask in the heat of their exhaust.

Almost as good, at least from Dewey's perspective, were the new sensor posts beside the front door, which beeped if you tried to leave without checking out your library materials. Dewey's new favorite place was just inside the left post. (Just like the left shoulder for the Dewey Carry. Was Dewey left-pawed?) He sat by that post for the first hour of every day, starting promptly at two minutes to nine. And that's where he greeted his friends, including Tony, our painter, who scratched the Dewkster whenever he came by, and Dewey's friend Doris Armstrong, who still brought him little gifts and surprises.

Dewey's friend Crystal moved away, but he still met the special education class every week. He even developed a relationship with Mark Carey, who owned the electronics store on the corner. Dewey knew Mark wasn't a cat lover, and he took fiendish delight in suddenly jumping on the table and scaring him. Mark took delight in bumping Dewey out of whatever chair he was lounging in—chairs were for patrons—even if there was nobody else in the library.

One morning I noticed a businessman in a suit sitting at a table, reading the *Wall Street Journal*. It looked like he had stopped in to kill time before a meeting, so I wasn't expecting to see a fluffy orange tail sticking out at his side. I looked closer and saw that Dewey had plopped down on his newspaper. Busy. Businessman.

Oh, Dewey, I thought, *you're pushing it now.* Then I realized the man was holding the newspaper with his right hand while petting Dewey with his left. One of them was purring; the other was smiling. That's when I knew Dewey had fallen into a comfort zone; nothing in that library could ever bother him.

That's why I was so surprised when I arrived at the library one morning to find Dewey pacing. When I opened the door, he ran a few steps, then stopped, waiting for me to follow.

"Do you need to go to the litter, Dewey? You know you don't have to wait for me."

It wasn't the litter, and he didn't have any interest in breakfast. He kept pacing back and forth, crying for me. Dewey never cried unless he was in pain, but I knew Dewey. He wasn't in pain.

I tried fixing his food. Nope. I checked to see if he had poop stuck in his fur. Poop in his fur drove him absolutely nuts—and there was no such thing as cat toilet paper. I checked his nose to see if he had a temperature, and his ears to see if he had an infection. Nothing.

"Let's make the rounds, Dew."

Like all cats, Dewey had hair balls. Whenever it happened, our fanatically neat cat was mortified.

But he had never acted this strangely, so I braced myself for the mother of all hair balls. I worked my way through fiction and nonfiction, checking every corner. But I didn't find anything.

Dewey was waiting for me in the children's section. The poor cat was in knots. But I didn't find anything there, either.

"I'm sorry, Dewey. I don't understand what you're trying to tell me."

When the staff arrived, I told them to keep an eye on Dewey. I was busy, and I couldn't spend all morning playing charades with a cat. If Dewey was still acting strangely in a few hours, I would take him to see Dr. Esterly.

Two minutes after the library opened, Jackie Shugars came back to my office. "You're not going to believe this, Vicki, but Dewey just peed on the cards."

I jumped up. "It can't be!"

To check out a book, we still stamped two cards. One went home with you in the book; the other went into a big bin with hundreds of other cards. When you returned the book, we pulled the corresponding card out of the bin and put the book back on the shelf. Sure enough, Dewey had peed in the front right corner of the bin.

I wasn't mad at Dewey. I was worried. He'd been in the library for years; he'd never acted out. This was completely out of character. But I didn't have long to think before one of our regular patrons came up and whispered in my ear, "You better get down here, Vicki. There's a bat in the children's section."

Sure enough, there it was: a bat, hanging by his heels behind a ceiling beam. And there was Dewey at *my* heels.

I tried to tell you. I tried to tell you. Now look what you've done. We could have taken care of this before anyone arrived. Now there are children in the library. I thought you were protecting them!

Have you ever been lectured by a cat? It's not a pleasant experience. Especially when the cat is right.

And especially when a bat is involved. I hate bats. I couldn't stand the thought of having one in the library, and I couldn't imagine being trapped all night with that thing flying all over the place. Poor Dewey.

"Don't worry, Dewey. Bats sleep during the day. He won't hurt anybody."

Dewey didn't look convinced, but I couldn't

worry about that now. I didn't want to scare the patrons, especially the children, so I quietly called the city janitor and told him, "Get down to the library right away. And bring your ladder."

He climbed up for a look. "It's a bat, all right."

"Shhh. Keep your voice down."

He climbed down. "You got a vacuum cleaner?"

I shivered. "Don't use the vacuum cleaner."

"How about Tupperware?"

I just stared at him. This was disgusting.

Someone said, "We've got an empty coffee can. It's got a lid."

The ordeal was over in a matter of seconds. The janitor just clapped the can over the bat and the bat was gone. Thank goodness. I mean, I really, really, really hate bats.

Now I had to sort out the mess in the cards.

"This is my fault," I told Jackie, who was still manning the circulation desk.

"I know." Jackie has a droll sense of humor.

"Dewey was trying to warn us. I'll clean this up."

"I figured you would."

I pulled out about twenty cards. Underneath them was a big pile of bat guano. Dewey hadn't just been trying to get my attention; he'd been using his scent to cover the stench of the intruder.

"Oh, Dewey, you must think I'm stupid."

He did. He really thought he was much smarter.

The next morning, Dewey started his sentry phase. Each morning, he sniffed three heating vents. He sniffed each one again after lunch. He knew those vents led somewhere and because of that, something might be able to get in. He had taken it upon himself to use his powerful nose to protect us. *If you can't even figure out there's a bat in the library,* he huffed, *how are you going to take care of all these people?*

I know, Dewey. You're right. I'm sorry. It's a good thing we have you.

CHAPTER 20

Puss in Books

Meanwhile, while we just went about our regular business in the library, Dewey's fame continued to grow. He was featured in all the cat magazines—*Cats, Cat Fancy, Cats & Kittens*. If the magazine had *cat* in the title, Dewey was probably in it. He even appeared in *Your Cat*, a leading British publication. Marti Attoun, a young freelance writer, traveled to Spencer with a photographer. Her article appeared in *American Profile*, a weekend insert in more than a thousand newspapers. Then, in the summer of 1996, a documentary filmmaker from Boston turned up in out-of-the-way Spencer, Iowa, camera in tow, ready to put Dewey in his first movie.

Gary Roma was traveling the country to create a documentary about library cats. He arrived expecting the kind of footage he'd shot at other libraries: cats darting behind bookshelves, walking away, sleeping, and doing everything possible to avoid looking into the camera. Dewey was exactly the opposite.

He didn't ham it up, but he went about all his usual activities, and he performed them on command. Gary arrived early in the morning to catch Dewey waiting for me at the front door. He shot Dewey sitting by the sensor posts greeting patrons; lying in his Buddha pose; playing with his favorite toys, Marty Mouse and the red yarn; sitting on a patron's shoulder in the Dewey Carry; and sleeping in a box.

Gary said, "This is the best footage I've shot so far. If you don't mind, I'll come back after lunch."

After lunch I sat down for an interview. After a few introductory questions, Gary asked, "What is the meaning of Dewey?"

I told him, "Dewey's great for the library. He

relieves stress. He makes it feel like home. People love him, especially children."

"Yes, but what's the deeper meaning?"

"There is no deeper meaning. Everyone enjoys spending time with Dewey. He makes us happy. What more to life is there than that?"

He kept pressing for meaning, meaning, *meaning*. Gary's first film was *Off the Ground & Off the Wall: A Doorstop Documentary*, and I could imagine him pressing all his subjects: "What does your doorstop mean to you?"

"It keeps the door from hitting the wall."

"Yes, but what about the deeper meaning?"

"Well, I can use it to hold the door open."

"Go deeper."

"Um, it keeps the room drafty?"

About six months after filming, we threw a party for the premiere showing of *Puss in Books*. The library was packed. The movie started with a distant shot of Dewey sitting on the floor of the Spencer library waving his tail slowly back and forth. As the camera zoomed in and followed him under a table, across some shelves, and finally to his favorite book cart for a ride, you heard my voice in the background:

We arrived at work one morning, and we went back to open the book drop and empty the books out, and there inside was this tiny little kitten. He was buried under tons of books, the book drop was just full of books. People will come in, and they'll hear the story of how we acquired Dewey, and they'll say, "Oh, you poor little thing. You were thrown into that book drop on that day.' And I'll say, 'Poor little thing, my foot. That was the luckiest day of that boy's life, because he's king around here, and he knows it."

As the last words rolled out, Dewey stared right into the camera, and boy, could you tell I was right. He really was the king.

By this time, I was used to strange calls about Dewey. The library was getting a couple of requests a week for interviews, and articles about our famous cat were turning up in our mail on an almost weekly basis. Dewey's official photograph (the one on the cover of this book) had appeared in magazines, newsletters, books, and newspapers from Minneapolis, Minnesota, to Jerusalem, Israel. It even appeared in a cat calendar; Dewey was Mr. January. But even I was surprised to receive a phone call from the Iowa office of a national pet food company.

"We've been watching Dewey," they said, "and we're impressed."

Who wouldn't be?

"He seems like an extraordinary cat. And obviously people love him."

You don't say!

"We'd like to use him in a print advertising campaign. We can't offer money, but we will provide free cat food for life."

I have to admit, I was tempted. Dewey was a finicky eater, and we were indulgent parents. We were throwing out dishes full of food every day just because he didn't like the smell, and we were donating a hundred cans of out-of-favor cat food a year. Most of the money for that food was coming out of my pocket. I was personally subsidizing the feeding of a good portion of the cats in Spencer.

"I'll talk to the library board," I said.

"We'll send over samples," the company replied.

By the time the next library board meeting rolled around, the decision had already been made. Not by me or the board, but by Dewey. Mr. Finicky completely rejected the free samples.

Are you kidding me? he told me with a disdainful sniff. *I can't work for this junk.*

"I'm sorry," I told the manufacturer. "Dewey only eats Fancy Feast."

CHAPTER 21

King of the Litter

Dewey's pickiness wasn't just a matter of personality. He had a disease. No, really, it's true. As digestive systems go, that poor cat really got a lemon.

Even when he was a kitten, Dewey hated being petted on the stomach. Stroke his back, scratch his ears, even pull his tail and poke him in the eye, but never pet his stomach. I didn't think much of it until Dr. Esterly tried to clean his back end when he was about two years old. "I'll just push down on the glands and squeeze them clean," he explained. "It will take thirty seconds."

Sounded easy enough. I held Dewey while Dr. Esterly prepared his equipment: a pair of rubber gloves and a paper towel. "Nothing to it, Dewey," I whispered. "It will be over before you know it."

But as soon as Dr. Esterly pressed down, Dewey screamed. This wasn't a mild complaint. This was a full-fledged, terrified cry. His body bolted like it had been hit by lightning, and his legs scrambled frantically. Then he threw his mouth over my finger and bit down. Hard.

Dr. Esterly looked at my finger. "He shouldn't have done that."

I rubbed the sore. "It's not a problem."

"Yes, it is a problem. A cat shouldn't bite like that."

I wasn't worried. That wasn't Dewey. I knew Dewey; he wasn't a biter. And I could still see the panic in the poor cat's eyes. He wasn't looking at anything. He was just staring. The pain had been blinding.

After that, Dewey truly hated Dr. Esterly. As soon as we pulled into the veterinary office's parking lot, he started shaking. The smell of the lobby sent him into uncontrollable tremors. He would bury his head in the crook of my arm as if to say, *Protect me.*

As soon as he heard Dr. Esterly's voice, Dewey

growled. Many cats hate the veterinarian in his office but treat him as any other human in the outside world. Not Dewey. He feared Dr. Esterly unconditionally. If he heard his voice in the library, Dewey growled and sprinted to the other side of the room. If Dr. Esterly managed to sneak up on him and reached out to pet him, Dewey sprang up, looked around in panic, and bolted away. I think he recognized Dr. Esterly's smell. Dewey had found his archenemy, and it happened to be one of the nicest men in town.

A few years later, Dewey started having trouble going to the bathroom. Some days, his litter box would have blood in it. Other days, he came tearing out of the back room like someone had lit a firecracker under his rear end.

Dr. Esterly diagnosed Dewey with constipation. Extreme constipation. "What kind of food does Dewey eat?"

I rolled my eyes. Dewey was the world's worst eater. "He's very picky," I said. "He has a remarkable sense of smell, so he can tell when the food is old or off in some way. Cat food isn't the highest quality, you know. It's just a bunch of leftover parts. So you can't blame him."

Dr. Esterly looked at me like a kindergarten teacher eyeing a parent who had just explained away her child's disruptive behavior.

"He always eats canned food?"

"Yes."

"Good. Does he drink water?"

"Never."

"Never?"

"The cat avoids his water dish like poison."

"More water," Dr. Esterly assured me. "That should clear up the problem."

Thanks, Doc, nothing to it. Except have you ever tried to get a cat to drink water against his will? It's impossible.

I started with gentle coaxing. Dewey turned away in disgust.

I tried bribery. "No food until you drink some water. Don't look at me like that. I can last longer than you can." But I couldn't. I always gave in.

I started petting Dewey as he ate. Slowly the petting turned to pushing. *If I force his head down into the water,* I thought, *he has to drink.* Needless to say, that plan didn't work.

Maybe it was the water. We tried warm water. We tried cold water. We tried refreshing the water every five minutes. We tried different faucets.

(Back then, there was no such thing as bottled water in Spencer, Iowa.) We tried putting ice in the water dish. Everyone likes ice water, right? Actually, the ice worked. Dewey took a lick. One lick. But otherwise, nothing. How could an animal stay alive without water?

Then one day I rounded the corner into the staff bathroom. There was Dewey, sitting on the toilet with his head completely buried in the bowl. All I could see was his rear end sticking straight up in the air. Toilet water! He was drinking toilet water! You sly cat!

Well, I thought, *at least he isn't going to get dehydrated.*

But that didn't help his constipation. Even though he drank toilet water, Dewey still couldn't go. When it got really bad, Dewey tended to hide. One morning, poor Sharon Joy reached into the top drawer of the circulation desk for a tissue, but instead grabbed a handful of hair. She literally fell out of her chair.

"How did he get in there?" she asked, staring down at Dewey's back. His head and rear were completely buried in the drawer.

Good question. The drawer hadn't been opened all morning, so Dewey must have climbed in during the night. I poked around under the desk. Sure enough, there was a small opening behind the drawers. But this was the top drawer, more than three feet off the ground. Mr. Rubber Spine had wiggled his way to the top of the crevice, turned a tight corner, and then curled up to sleep in a space no bigger than a cupcake.

I tried to wake him. Dewey shrugged me off and didn't move. This wasn't like him. Obviously something was wrong. Off to the vet's office!

It turns out Dewey had a disease. (See, I told you.) It was called megacolon, and it was extremely rare. If Dewey had lived in the alley, his disease would have shortened his life. In the library, I could expect periodic but severe bouts of constipation, accompanied by very picky eating. So now Dewey had an excuse for not liking his food. That cat had it all figured out, didn't he?

Dr. Esterly suggested an expensive cat food, the kind you could buy only from a veterinarian. I forget the name, maybe Middle-aged Cat with Tummy Troubles Formula? The bill almost broke the budget. I hated to dish out thirty dollars for something I knew wasn't going to work.

I told Dr. Esterly, "Dewey's not going to like this."

"Put it in his bowl. Don't give him anything else. He'll eat it. No cat will starve itself to death."

I put the fancy new food in the bowl, just like Dr. Esterly said. Dewey didn't eat it, just like I thought. He sniffed it once and walked away.

This food, it's no good. I want the usual, please.

The next day, he dropped the subtle approach. Instead of sniffing and walking away, he sat down by the food bowl and cried.

Whhhyyyy? What have I done to deserve this?

"Sorry, Dewey. Doctor's orders."

After two days, he was weak, but he wouldn't even bat the food with his paw. That's when I realized Dewey was stubborn. He was a mellow cat. He was accommodating. But when it came to an important principle like food, Dewey would never roll over and play dog.

And neither would I. Mom could be stubborn, too.

So Dewey went behind my back. First he hit up Sharon Joy by jumping on her desk and rubbing her arm.

When that didn't work, he tried his old friend Joy. Then he tried Audrey, Cynthia, Paula, every librarian, right down the line. He tried Kay, even though he knew she was the no-nonsense type.

Kay was a farm girl, and she had no time for weakness. But I could see even she was beginning to waver. She tried to act tough, but she was developing a real warm spot in her heart for the Dew.

I didn't care. Let them disapprove. I was going to win this round. It might break my heart now, but in the end Dewey would thank me. And besides, I was Mommy, and I said so!

On the fourth day, even the patrons turned on me. "Just feed him, Vicki! He's so hungry." Dewey had been shamelessly putting on a starving cat act for his fans, and it was clearly working.

Finally, on the fifth day, I caved and gave Dewey his favorite can of Fancy Feast. He gobbled it down without even coming up for air. *That's it,* he said, licking his lips and then stepping to the corner for a long tongue bath of his face and ears. *We all feel better now, don't we?*

That night I went out and bought him an armful of cans. I couldn't fight anymore. *Better a constipated cat,* I thought, *than a starving one.*

For two months Dewey was happy. I was happy. All was right with the world.

Then Dewey decided he didn't like Fancy Feast, chunky chicken flavor. He wasn't going to eat another bite of Fancy Feast, chunky chicken flavor. He wanted something new, thank you very much. I bought a new flavor, something in the moist smelly blob category. Dewey took one sniff and walked away. *Nope, not that one, either.*

"You'll eat it, young man, or no dessert for you."

At the end of the day, the food was still there, dried out and crusty. What was I supposed to do? The cat was sick! It took five tries, but I found a flavor he liked. It only lasted a few weeks. Then he wanted something new. Oh boy. The Library King was really getting fussy now!

Soon, the situation was completely absurd. How could you not laugh at an entire bookshelf full of cat food? I'm not exaggerating. We kept Dewey's items on two shelves in the staff area, and one of them was only for food. We had at least five flavors on hand at all times. The Dew had Midwestern taste. His favorite flavors were beef, chunky chicken, beef and liver, and turkey, but you never knew when another flavor would strike his fancy. He hated seafood, but he fell in love with shrimp. For a week. Then he wouldn't touch it.

Even worse, Dewey was still constipated, so on Dr. Esterly's orders I copied a page out of a calendar and hung it on the wall. Every time someone found a present in Dewey's litter box, they marked the date. The calendar was known throughout the office as Dewey's Poop Chart.

When Dewey hadn't gone for three days, we locked him in the back closet with his litter. Dewey hated being locked anywhere, especially a closet.

"It's for your own good, Dew."

After a half hour, I let him out. If no evidence turned up in the litter box, I locked him in for another half hour. No poop, back in the box. Three times was the limit. After three times, he wasn't holding out; he really couldn't go.

This strategy completely backfired. Dewey soon became so pampered he refused to use the litter unless someone took him to the box. He stopped going completely at night, which meant first thing in the morning I had to carry him— yes, carry him—to his litter.

Talk about being the king!

CHAPTER 22

Dewey's Gift

I know, I know. I was a sucker. A spoiler of cats. You should never get in the habit of carrying your cat to the litter box like I carried Dewey. Because if you do, they are going to expect to be carried to their litter every day for the rest of their life.

But Dewey... well, Dewey was a little different. Yes, he expected to be carried, but he gave me something in return. Something I really needed.

You see, about the same time as Dewey's Poop Chart, I got really sick. So sick I worried that I might not be able to work at the library anymore. Everybody knew I was sick, but nobody knew the extent of my pain: not my parents, my friends, not even my daughter, Jodi. The only person that seemed to understand, in his way, was Dewey.

Whenever I had needed him in the past, Dewey had always been by my side. He had perched on my computer at night in the lonely library, and he had sat beside me on the sofa and waited for Jodi. Now he moved from sitting beside me to sitting on my lap. He stopped walking beside me and started insisting on climbing into my arms. That might seem like a small thing, but it made all the difference to me because, you see, I didn't have anybody to touch. There was no one to hug me, to tell me it was going to be okay.

For two years, Dewey touched me every day. He put his head on me. He snuggled in my arms. He seemed to understand that love was constant, but that it could be raised to a higher level when it really mattered.

Every morning since his first week in the library, Dewey had waited for me at the front door. He would stare at me, then turn and run for his food bowl when I opened the door. Then, as I said, he started wanting to be carried to his litter box. And then, on one of the worst mornings of that terrible two years, he did something else: he started waving.

Yes, waving. He was standing at the front door to the library waving.

I stopped and looked at him. He stopped and looked at me. Then he started waving again.

It happened the next morning, too. And the next. And the next, until finally I understood this was our new routine. For the rest of his life, as soon as Dewey saw my car pull into the parking lot, he started scratching his left paw on the front door. The wave continued as I crossed the street and approached the door.

It wasn't frantic. He wasn't meowing or pacing. He was sitting very still and waving at me, as if welcoming me to the library and, at the same time, reminding me he was there. As if I could ever forget. Every morning, Dewey waving at me as I walked toward the library made me feel better: about the job, about life, about myself. If Dewey was waving, everything was all right.

"Good morning, Dewey," I would say, with a smile on my face, even on the darkest and coldest mornings. He would rub against my ankle. My buddy. My boy. Then I would cradle him in my arms and carry him to his litter box like a king. Yes, I was a spoiler of cats. But how could I deny him that?

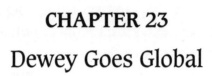

CHAPTER 23

Dewey Goes Global

Of course, I wasn't the only one smitten with King Dewey. As part of my job, I taught courses to other librarians remotely, using a web camera and a videoconferencing system. Every time I sat down to teach the opening class of a course, the first question was, "Where's Dewey?"

"Yes," another librarian would pipe up, "can we see him?"

Fortunately, Dewey attended all meetings at the Spencer Public Library. He preferred meetings of actual people, of course, but teleconferences were acceptable, too. For my courses, he'd lounge in the center of the table waiting for me to push a button and make him appear on viewing screens all over the state. As soon as I did, you could probably hear the gasp in Nebraska.

"He's so cute."

"Do you think my library should get a cat?"

"Only if it's the right cat." That's what I always told them. "You can't get just any cat. He has to be special."

"Special?"

"Calm, patient, dignified, intelligent, and above all, outgoing. A library cat has to love people. It also helps if he's gorgeous and comes with an unforgettable story." I didn't mention that he had to be loving and absolutely love, with his whole heart, being the library cat.

I looked over at my big orange buddy. "You're loving this, aren't you?"

He gave me an innocent look. *Who, me? I'm just doing my job.*

It wasn't just librarians who loved Dewey. I was working in my office one morning when Kay called me to the front desk. Standing there was a family of four, two young parents and their children.

"This nice family," Kay said, "is from Rhode Island. They've come to meet Dewey."

Rhode Island. That was about two thousand miles away!

The father extended his hand. "We were in Minneapolis, so we decided to rent a car and drive down. The kids just love Dewey."

Was this man crazy? Minneapolis was five hours away!

"Wonderful," I said, shaking their hands. "How did you find out about Dewey?"

"We read about him in *Cats* magazine. We're cat lovers."

Obviously.

"Okay," I said, because I couldn't think of anything else. "Let's go meet him."

Dewey was, thank goodness, as eager to please as always. He played with the children. He posed for photographs. I showed the little girl the Dewey Carry, and she walked him all around the library on her left shoulder (always the left). I don't know if it was worth the nine-hour round trip, but the family left happy.

"That was weird," Kay said once the family was gone.

"It sure was. I bet that never happens again."

It happened again. And again. And again. And again. They came from Utah, Washington,

Mississippi, California, Maine, and every other corner of the map. Older couples, younger couples, families. I wish I had thought to write down their names, but I didn't. At first it seemed so unlikely that more people would come. So, why bother? By the time we realized the Dew's appeal, the visitors no longer seemed unusual.

How were these people finding out about Dewey? I had no idea. The library never pursued publicity for Dewey. We never contacted a single newspaper, with the exception of the *Spencer Daily Reporter*. We never hired a publicity agent or marketing manager. After the Shopko cutest pet win, we never entered Dewey in any other contests.

We were Dewey's answering service, nothing more. We just picked up the phone, and there was another magazine, another television program, another radio station wanting an interview. Or we opened the mail and found an article about Dewey from a magazine we'd never heard of or a newspaper halfway across the country. A week later, another family popped up at the library.

Dewey's visitors all left smitten. I know this not only because they told me and because I saw their eyes and their smiles, but because they went home and told people about Dewey. They showed them the pictures. At first they sent letters to friends and relatives. Later, they sent e-mails. He received letters from Taiwan, Holland, South Africa, Norway, Australia. He had pen pals in half a dozen countries. A ripple started in a little town in northwest Iowa, and somehow word of mouth carried it all over the world.

The visitors who truly touched me, though, were the young parents from Texas and their six-year-old daughter. As soon as they entered the library, it was clear this was a special trip for her. Was she sick? Was she sad? Had she lost something? I don't know, but I had the feeling the parents had offered her one wish, and this was it. The girl wanted to meet Dewey. And, I noticed, she had brought a present.

"It's a toy mouse," her father told me. He was smiling, but I could tell he was worried. This was no ordinary spur-of-the-moment visit.

As I smiled back at him, only one thought was going through my mind: "I hope that toy mouse has catnip in it." Dewey would regularly go through periods where he wanted nothing to do with any toy that didn't contain catnip. Unfortunately, this was one of those times.

All I said was, "I'll go get Dewey."

Dewey was asleep in his new fake fur–lined bed, which we kept outside my office door in front of a heating unit. As I woke him up I tried a little mental telepathy: *Please, Dewey, please. This one's important.* He was so tired, he barely opened his eyes.

The little girl was hesitant, as many children are, so the mother petted Dewey first. Dewey lay there like a sack of potatoes. When the girl finally reached out to pet him, Dewey woke up enough to lean into her hand. The father put both Dewey and the girl on his lap. Dewey immediately snuggled up against her.

They sat like that for a minute or two. Finally the girl showed Dewey the present she had brought, carefully tied with a ribbon and bow. Dewey perked up, but I could tell he was still tired. He would have preferred to snooze in the girl's lap all morning. *Come on, Dewey,* I thought. *Snap out of it.* The girl unwrapped the gift, and sure enough, it was a plain toy mouse, no catnip. My heart sank. This was going to be a disaster.

The girl dangled the mouse in front of Dewey's sleepy eyes to get his attention. Then she deli-cately tossed it a few feet away. As soon as it hit the ground, Dewey jumped on it. He chased that toy; he threw it in the air; he batted it with his paws. The girl giggled with delight. Dewey never played with it again, but while that little girl was here, he loved that mouse. He gave that mouse every ounce of energy he had. And the little girl beamed. She just beamed. She had come hundreds of miles to see a cat, and she was not disappointed. Why did I ever worry about Dewey? He always came through.

DEWEY'S JOB DESCRIPTION

WRITTEN IN RESPONSE TO THE QUESTION, "SO WHAT IS DEWEY'S JOB?", WHICH WAS OFTEN ASKED AFTER PEOPLE FOUND OUT DEWEY RECEIVED A 15% LIBRARY EMPLOYEE DISCOUNT FROM DR. ESTERLY.

1 Reducing stress for all humans who pay attention to him.

2 Sitting by the front door every morning at nine to greet the public as they enter the library.

3 Sampling all boxes that enter the library for security problems and comfort level.

4 Attending all meetings in the Round Room as official library ambassador.

5 Providing comic relief for staff and visitors.

6 Climbing in book bags and briefcases while patrons are studying or trying to retrieve needed papers.

7 Generating free national and worldwide publicity for Spencer Public Library. (This entails sitting still for photographs, smiling for the camera, and generally being cute.)

8 Working toward status as world's most finicky cat by refusing all but the most expensive, delectable foods.

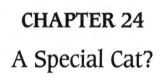

CHAPTER 24

A Special Cat?

I've always wondered: What makes people special? What makes them important?

Often times, it seems, people believe that to be special you have to *do* something— something "in your face" and caught on camera. We like it when a newsworthy town survives a tornado or produces a president. We want an important child to be a star athlete or the smartest kid in the state. And we expect a famous cat to save a child from a burning building, find his way home after being left behind on the other side of the country, or meow "The Star-Spangled Banner."

Dewey wasn't like that. He was like one of those seemingly ordinary people who turn out to be different. He didn't perform spectacular feats. He didn't do one heroic thing; he did something important every single day.

Dewey came from humble beginnings (an Iowa alley); he survived tragedy (a freezing drop box); he found his place (a small-town library). His passion was to make that place, no matter how small and out of the way, a better place for everyone. He spent his time changing lives in Spencer, Iowa, one lap at a time. He never left anyone out, and he never took anyone for granted.

Surely you know Wilbur, the pig in *Charlotte's Web*. Dewey had that personality: enthusiastic, honest, charming, radiant, humble (for a cat), and above all, he was a friend. He wasn't just another cat for people to pet and smile about. Every regular user of the library, *every single one*, felt they had a unique relationship with Dewey.

Like Sharon and Tony's daughter, Emmy, who had Down syndrome and sometimes came on Sunday mornings to see Dewey. Every Saturday night Emmy asked, "Is tomorrow a Dewey day?" The first thing Emmy did every "Dewey day" was search for Dewey. When he was younger, he would usually be waiting by the door, but as he aged, Emmy often found him lying in the sun by a window. She would pick him up and bring him to her mommy so they could pet him together. "Hi, Dewey. I love you," Emmy would say in a soft, kind voice, the way her own mother talked to her. For Emmy, that was the voice of love.

Yvonne Barry, a single woman in her late thirties, came to the library three or four times a week. Every time, Dewey tried to coax her to open the bathroom door for him. Once inside, he'd jump on the sink and beg for the water to be turned on.

He didn't drink this water. He watched it. Something about the way it bounced off the drain plug fascinated him. He'd stare at that water, then suddenly take a quick slap at it with his paw. Watch, watch, watch...slap. Watch, watch, watch...slap. Yvonne would wait for him to finish, then open the door so he could leave. It was their ritual.

But on the day Yvonne had to put her own cat to sleep, Dewey sat with her for more than two hours without asking for a thing. He didn't know what had happened, but he knew something was wrong. Years later, when she told me that story, I could tell it was still important to her.

This is not to say everyone knew Dewey. No matter how famous and popular Dewey became, there was always someone with no idea the Spencer Public Library had a cat. A family would drive from Nebraska to see Dewey. They would bring gifts, spend two hours playing with him and taking pictures. Ten minutes after they left, someone would come up to the desk, obviously worried, and whisper, "I don't want to alarm you, but there's a cat in the library."

"I know," we would whisper back. "He lives here. He's the world's most famous library cat."

"Oh," they'd say with a smile. "Then I guess you already know."

CHAPTER 25

Home Is Where
the Books Are

It wasn't until he turned thirteen years old—about seventy in human years—that I noticed for the first time the Dew was mellowing. He spent more time in his cat bed, and strenuous play was replaced by quiet book cart rides. Instead of jumping onto the cart, he would meow for us to pick him up so he could ride at the front of the cart like the captain of a ship. He stopped jumping to the ceiling lights, more out of boredom, I believe, than physical necessity.

When Dewey gave up walking the top of the bookcases, Kay took his old cat bed and put it on a shelf above her desk. Dewey would snuggle up in that bed and watch Kay work. One day not too long after Kay set up the new arrangement,

Dewey jumped up to his bed and the shelf collapsed. The cat flew one way, four legs flailing. Notepads and paper clips flew the other. Before the last paper clip had hit the floor, Dewey was back to survey the damage.

"Not scared of too much in this library, are you?" Kay joked with a smile.

Only the brush and the bath, Dewey would have said if he was being honest. The older Dewey got, the more he hated being brushed and bathed.

He also didn't have as much patience for preschool children, who tended to poke and pull at him. He had always loved children, and he always would, but their roughness was getting harder and harder on his old bones. He was stiffening up, and he could no longer tolerate the small knocks and bruises. He never lashed out at children, and he rarely ran from them. He simply began to scoot away and hide when certain children came looking for him.

Babies were a different story. One day I watched Dewey plop himself down a few feet from an infant girl who was on the floor in a baby carrier. For a full minute, Dewey just sat with a bored expression, looking off into the distance as if to say, *Just happened to be walking by*. Then, when he thought I wasn't looking, he squirmed an inch closer. *Just adjusting my position,* his body language said, *nothing to see here.* A minute later, he did it again. Then again.

Slowly, inch by inch, he crept closer, until finally he was pressed right up against the carrier. He popped his head over the edge, as if to confirm the child was inside. The infant reached her little hand over the edge and snatched his ear. Dewey adjusted his head so she could get a better grip. She laughed, kicking her legs and squeezing his ear. And boy, did she squeeze. Hard. Dewey sat quietly, a contented look on his face.

He was never one to judge. That was one of the best things about Dewey. When he was a kitten, he spent time each day with a homeless woman who came in to pet him. As an older cat, one of his best friends was a homeless man who started appearing at the library every day. The man was unshaven, uncombed, and unwashed. He never said a word to anyone. He never looked at anyone. It was clear he wanted only one thing: Dewey. He would pick Dewey up and drape him over his left shoulder; Dewey would lie there, purring, for twenty minutes, while the man patted him gently.

Our new assistant children's librarian, Donna Stanford, had recently returned to northwest Iowa and didn't know anyone in town. The only local resident who reached out to Donna was Dewey. He loved to ride on her shoulder while she rolled around in her office chair shelving books. When he tired of that, he would climb down onto her lap so Donna could pet him. Sometimes she read him children's books. I caught them by surprise one day, Dewey resting with his eyes closed, Donna deep in thought. I could tell she was startled.

"Don't worry," I said. "It is part of your job description to hold the kitty."

Then there was my daughter Jodi's boyfriend, Scott. The first time he came to Spencer, Jodi and I took Scott to the library to meet Dewey. That's when I knew this relationship was serious; Jodi had never introduced Dewey to one of her boyfriends before.

Dewey was overjoyed to see Jodi. He may have been old, but he still did backflips for that girl! Scott gave the two of them time together, then gently picked Dewey up and petted him. Not on the stomach, which Dewey hated, but along the back. He walked him around the empty library in the Dewey Carry. He pulled out his camera and took a snapshot for his mother. She had heard the Dewey stories, and she was a big fan. Seeing Scott with Dewey, and Dewey with Scott, told me everything I needed to know.

It never occurred to me there was anything unusual about my grown daughter taking her boyfriend to the library to meet her mother's cat. After all, Dewey was more special to me than any animal I had ever known. He was more special to me than I ever believed an animal could be. We had chosen to live our lives together, he and I, not just tomorrow, but forever.

Dewey the cat was part of my family; his opinion mattered. How could anyone seriously consider being a part of this family without knowing him? But all those feelings didn't change a fundamental truth: Dewey belonged in the library. His place was with the public.

Dewey was happy at my house for a day or two whenever it was a holiday, but as soon as we got in the car and headed downtown to the library...oh boy, that cat came alive. He'd put his front feet on the dashboard and stare out the window. I had to take the turns slowly, or he'd slide right off and fall face first on the floor. He was almost shaking with anticipation.

When he smelled Sister's Café, Dewey knew we were a few blocks away. That's when he got really excited. He'd move to the armrest and put his paws on the side window, like he was trying to push the door open. *We're here! We're here!* He'd look over his shoulder and practically yell it to me when we entered the alley. As soon as the door opened, he jumped into my arms and I carried him across the threshold.

And then...bliss.

There was nothing Dewey loved more than being home.

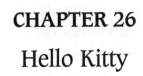

CHAPTER 26

Hello Kitty

We received the e-mail in early 2003, when Dewey was fifteen. I had to read it twice, just to make sure. Yes, it was true. Japanese Public Television wanted to film Dewey! They were planning a documentary, and they had discovered Dewey through a feature in the Japanese magazine *Nekobiyori*. Would we mind if a film crew came to Spencer for a day?

That's funny, we had no idea Dewey had appeared in a Japanese magazine!

A few months later, six people from Tokyo, Japan, arrived at the Spencer Public Library. They had flown to Des Moines, rented a van, and driven to Spencer. Iowa in May is beautiful. The corn is just below eye level, three or four feet tall, so you can see the fields spreading into the distance. Of course, it's two hundred miles from Des Moines to Spencer, and that's all you can see. What were six people from Tokyo thinking after three and a half hours of looking at corn? We'd have to ask them, because they were probably the only people from Tokyo ever to make that drive.

The crew had one day to film, so they asked me to arrive at the library before seven. It was a miserably rainy morning. The interpreter, the only woman in the group, asked me to open the first set of doors so they could set up their cameras in the lobby. As they were carting equipment, around the corner came Dewey. He was half-asleep, stretching his back legs as cats often do when they first wake up. When he saw me, he trotted over and gave me a wave. *Oh, it's you. What are you doing here so early? I wasn't expecting you for twenty minutes.* You could have set your watch by that cat.

Once the crew set up the cameras, the interpreter said, "We'd like him to wave again."

Oh, brother. I tried to explain, as best I could, that Dewey waved only once, when he saw me first thing in the morning. The director, Mr. Hoshi, wouldn't hear of it. He was used not only to giving orders but to having them obeyed. He was definitely the man in charge. And right now, he wanted that wave.

So I went back to my car and approached the library again, pretending I hadn't been in that morning. Dewey just stared at me.

What? You were just here five minutes ago.

I entered the library, turned on the lights, turned off the lights, went back to the car, waited five minutes, and approached the library again. Mr. Hoshi thought this might fool Dewey into thinking it was the next day.

It didn't.

We tried for an hour to get footage of Dewey waving. Finally I said, "Look, the poor cat has been sitting there this whole time waiting for his food. I have to feed him." Mr. Hoshi agreed. I scooped Dewey up and rushed to the litter box. The last thing I wanted the Japanese to get on film was flying poop. Dewey relieved himself, then ate a leisurely breakfast. By the time he was finished, the camera crew was set up inside. They had come halfway around the world, and they never got their wave.

But they got everything else. Dewey was slowing down, but he hadn't lost his enthusiasm for strangers. Especially strangers with cameras. He greeted each member of the crew with a rub on the leg; one cameraman even laid his camera on the floor for a Dewey-eye view. Then the interpreter politely asked me to put Dewey on a bookshelf. He sat there and let them film. He jumped from shelf to shelf. Then she said, "Have him walk down the shelf between the books and jump off the end."

I thought, *Wait a second. He's a cat, not a trained animal in the circus, and that's a pretty specific request. I hope you didn't come all this way expecting a show because there's no way he's going to walk that shelf, slalom between the display books, and jump off at command.*

I trudged down to the far end of the shelf and called, "Come here, Dewey." Dewey walked down the shelf, squeezed between the books, and jumped down to my feet.

Amazing.

Anything else? Oh yes, much more. For five hours Mr. Hoshi gave orders and Dewey complied. He sat on a computer. He sat on a table. He sat on the floor with his feet crossed and stared into the camera. He rode on his favorite book cart with his feet hanging down through the openings, completely relaxed. No time to dally; move, move, move.

A three-year-old girl and her mother agreed to appear in the film, so I put Dewey on the glider chair with them. The girl was nervous, grabbing and pulling at Dewey. Dewey didn't mind. He sat through the whole five-minute ordeal and never forgot to stare sweetly at the camera.

I had told the interpreter that people came from all over the United States to visit Dewey, but I don't think Mr. Hoshi believed me. Then, just after lunch, in walked a family from New Hampshire. Talk about timing! The family was at a wedding in Des Moines and decided to rent a car and drive up to see Dewey. Again, that's a three-and-a-half-hour drive!

Mr. Hoshi interviewed the visitors. He took footage of them shooting their own footage of Dewey with their camcorder. I taught the girl, who was five or six, the Dewey Carry, and how to gently rock back and forth until he put his head down on her back and closed his eyes. The family stayed an hour; the Japanese crew left soon after. As soon as they were gone, Dewey fell asleep and was out the rest of the day.

We received two copies of the DVD. The electronics store on the corner loaned us a giant television, and we packed the library for a special viewing. By this time, Dewey had been on the radio in Canada and New Zealand. He had appeared in newspapers and magazines in dozens of countries. His photograph had been all over the world. But this was different. This was worldwide television!

I had sneaked a peek at the video, so I was a little nervous. The documentary was an alphabetic trip through the world of cats. There were twenty-six featured cats, one for each letter of the alphabet. Yes, our alphabet, even though the documentary was in Japanese. Weird, right?

I told the audience, "There are a lot of other cats in this documentary. Dewey is near the end, and the whole thing is in Japanese, so let's take a vote. Should we fast-forward to Dewey's part or watch the whole thing?"

"Watch the whole thing! Watch the whole thing!"

Ten minutes late the crowd was shouting, "Fast-forward! Fast-forward!" Let's just say it was extremely boring to watch cats sitting around and interviews we couldn't understand.

When we hit the letter *W*, a cry went up around the room, no doubt waking the snoozers. There was our Dewey, along with the words *Working Cat* in English and Japanese. There I was, walking up to the library in the rain, while the announcer said something in Japanese. We understood only three words: "America, Iowa-shun, Spencer." Another loud cheer. A few seconds later we heard: "Dewey a-Deedamore Booksa!"

And there was Dewey, sitting at the front door (I have to admit, a wave would have been nice), followed by Dewey sitting on a bookshelf, Dewey walking through two bookshelves, Dewey sitting, and sitting, and sitting and being petted by a little boy under a table and...sitting. One and a half minutes, and it was over. No little girl with Dewey on her lap. No riding the shoulder. No book cart. No family from New Hampshire. They didn't even use the shot of Dewey walking on top of the bookshelf, squeezing between the books, and jumping off the end. They came halfway around the world for a minute and a half of sitting.

There was silence in the library. Stunned silence.

And then a huge burst of cheering. Our Dewey was an international star. Here was the proof. So what if we didn't have a clue what the announcer was saying? So what if Dewey's scene was barely longer than a typical commercial break? There was our library. There was our librarian. There was our Dewey. And the announcer definitely said, "America, Iowa-shun, Spencer."

The town of Spencer has never forgotten that Japanese documentary. We have two copies in the library, but nobody ever watches them. *Puss in Books* is much more popular. But the fact that a film crew came from Tokyo to Spencer? That's something we'll never forget. The local radio station and the newspaper both ran long features, and for months people came into the library to talk about it.

"What was the crew like?"

"What did they eat?"

"Where did they go while in town?"

"What else did they film?"

"Can you believe it?"

"Can you believe it?"

"Can you believe it?"

Of course, Spencer residents aren't the only ones who remember that documentary. After it aired, we received several letters from Japan and forty requests for Dewey postcards. Our library website tallies the origin of online visitors, and for years after the documentary aired, Japan was the second most popular country of origin, after the United States.

Somehow, I don't think those Japanese visitors were interested in checking out our books. They were interested in checking out our Dewey.

CHAPTER 27

The Library Lion

I realized Dewey was losing his hearing when he stopped responding to the word *bath*. For years, that word had sent him into a scamper. The staff would be talking, and someone would say, "I had to clean my bathtub last night."

Bam, Dewey was gone. Every time.

"That isn't about you, Dewey!"

But he wasn't listening. Say the word *bath*—or *brush* or *comb* or *scissors* or *doctor* or *vet*—and Dewey disappeared. Especially if Kay or I said them. When I was away on library business or out sick, Kay took care of Dewey. If he needed something, even comfort or love, and I wasn't around, he went to Kay. She may have been distant at first, but after all those years she had become his second mother, the one who loved him but wouldn't tolerate his bad habits. If Kay and I were standing together and even thought the word *water*, Dewey ran.

Then one day someone said *bath* and he didn't run. Hmm. Interesting. I started to watch him more closely. Sure enough, he had stopped running away every time a truck rumbled by in the alley behind the library. The sound of the back door opening used to send him sprinting to sniff the incoming boxes; now, he wasn't moving at all. He wasn't jumping at sudden loud noises, and he wasn't coming as often when patrons called. That, however, might not have had much to do with hearing.

Dewey was seventeen years old—which is like being about eighty-five in human years. He still greeted everyone at the front door. He still searched out laps, but on his own terms. He had arthritis in his back left hip, and jostling him in the wrong place or picking him up the wrong way would cause him to limp away in pain.

More and more in the late morning and afternoon he sat on the circulation desk, where he was protected by staff. He was supremely confident in his beauty and popularity; he knew patrons would come to him. He looked like a lion surveying his kingdom. He even sat like a lion, with his paws crossed in front of him and his back legs tucked underneath, a model of dignity and grace.

The staff started quietly suggesting that patrons be gentle with Dewey. Joy, especially, became very protective of him. She often brought her nieces and nephews to see Dewey, so she knew how rough people could be. "These days," she would tell the patrons, "Dewey prefers a gentle pet on the head."

Even the elementary school children understood Dewey was an old man now, and they were sensitive to his needs. This was his second generation of Spencer children; their parents were the children who had gotten to know Dewey when he was a kitten. Now they were all grown up! And they made sure their kids were well behaved. When the children touched him gently, Dewey would lie against their legs or, if they were sitting on the floor, on their laps. But rough petting often drove him away.

"That's all right, Dew," I'd reassure him. "Whatever you need."

After years of trial and error, we had finally found our finicky cat an acceptable bed. It was small, with white fake fur sides and an electric warmer in the bottom. We kept it in front of the wall heater outside my office. Dewey loved nothing more than lounging in his bed with the heating pad turned all the way up.

In the winter, when the wall heater was on, he would get so warm he had to throw himself over the side and roll around on the floor. His fur was so hot you couldn't even touch it. He would lie on his back for ten minutes with all his legs spread to let the heat out. If a cat could pant, Dewey would have been panting. As soon as he was cool, he climbed back into his bed in front of the heater and started the process all over again.

Heat wasn't Dewey's only indulgence. I may have been a sucker for Dewey's whims, but our assistant children's librarian, Donna, was spoiling him rotten. If Dewey didn't eat his food right away, she heated it in the microwave for him. If he still didn't eat it, she threw it out and opened another can. Donna didn't trust ordinary flavors. Why should Dewey eat gizzards and toes?

Donna drove to Milford, fifteen miles away, because a little store there sold exotic cat food. She bought duck. Dewey was fond of that for a week. She tried lamb, too, but nothing stuck for very long. Donna kept trying new flavor after new flavor and new can after new can.

Despite our best efforts, though, Dewey was thinning down, so at his next checkup Dr. Franck prescribed a series of medicines to fatten him up. That's right, you heard it, Dewey had a new vet. He had outlasted his old nemesis, Dr. Esterly, who had retired and donated his practice to a nonprofit animal advocacy group.

Along with his medicine, Dr. Franck gave me a pill shooter that, theoretically, shot the pills so far down Dewey's throat that he couldn't spit them out. But Dewey was smart. He took his pill so calmly I thought, *Good, we made it. That was easy.* He'd wait five minutes until I stopped watching him. Then he'd sneak behind a shelf somewhere and cough the pill back up. I found little white pills all over the library.

I didn't force Dewey's to take his medicine. He

was eighteen now (which meant about ninety); if he didn't want medicine, he didn't have to take it. Instead, I bought him a container of yogurt and started giving him a lick every day.

That opened the floodgates. Kay started giving him bites of cold cuts out of her sandwiches. Joy started sharing her ham sandwich; pretty soon Dewey was following her to the kitchen whenever he saw her walk through the door with a bag in her hand. One day Sharon left a sandwich unwrapped on her desk. When she came back a minute later, the top slice of bread had been carefully turned over and placed to the side. The bottom slice of bread was sitting exactly where it had been, untouched. But all the meat was gone.

After Thanksgiving 2005, we discovered Dewey loved turkey, so the staff began saving holiday scraps. We tried to freeze them, but he could always tell when the turkey wasn't fresh. Dewey never lost his keen sense of smell. That's one reason I scoffed when Sharon offered Dewey a bite of garlic chicken, her favorite lunch. I told her, "No way Dewey is going to eat garlic. It's too spicy."

He ate every bite. Who was this cat? For eighteen years, Dewey ate nothing but specific brands and flavors of cat food. Now, he'd eat anything.

I thought, *If we can fatten Dewey up on human food, why not? Isn't that better than a pill?*

I bought him braunschweiger, a cold loaf of sliced liver sausage many people around here consider a delicacy. Braunschweiger is about 80 percent pure fat. If anything would fatten Dewey up, it was braunschweiger. He wouldn't touch it.

What Dewey really wanted was Arby's Beef 'n' Cheddar sandwiches. He gobbled them down. Inhaled them. He didn't even chew the beef; he just sucked it in. I don't know what was in those sandwiches, but once he started on Arby's Beef 'n' Cheddar, Dewey's digestion improved. His constipation decreased. He started eating two cans of cat food a day, and because the Arby's food was so salty, he was slurping down a full dish of water as well. He even started using the litter box on his own.

But Dewey didn't have a couple of owners, he had hundreds, and most of them couldn't see the improvements. All they saw was the cat they loved getting thinner and thinner. Dewey never hesitated to play up his condition. He was a real trickster. He would sit on the circulation desk, and whenever someone approached to pet him, he would whine. They always fell for it.

"What's the matter, Dewey?"

He'd lead them toward his food dish. He'd look forlornly at the food, then back at them, and, with his big eyes full of sorrow, drop his head.

"Vicki! Dewey's hungry!"

"He has a can of food in the bowl."

"But he doesn't like it."

"That's his second flavor this morning. I threw the first can away an hour ago."

"But he's crying. Look at him. He just flopped down on the floor."

"We can't just give him cans of food all day."

"What about something else?"

"He ate an Arby's sandwich this morning."

"Look at him. He's so thin. You have to be feed him more."

"Don't worry, we're taking good care of him."

"But he's so thin. Can't you give him something for me?"

I could...except Dewey did the same thing yesterday. And the day before that. And the day before that. In fact, you're the fifth person he's hit with the starving-cat routine today.

Now, how was I going to tell a patron that? I always gave in, which of course just encouraged more bad behavior. I think Dewey enjoyed the taste of food more when he knew I didn't want to give it to him.

Let's call it the taste of victory.

CHAPTER 28

Don't Judge a Cat by His Fur

As Dewey entered old age, the kindness of Spencer Public Library patrons really began to show. Friends and visitors alike were gentler around him. They talked to him more and were attentive to his needs. Occasionally someone would comment that he looked weak, or thin, or dirty, but I knew they were concerned because they loved him and wanted him to be well.

"What's wrong with his fur?" was probably the most common question.

"Nothing," I told them. "He's just old."

It's true, Dewey's fur had lost much of its luster. It was no longer radiant orange, but a dull copper. It was also increasingly matted, so much so

I couldn't keep up with a simple brushing. I took Dewey to Dr. Franck, who explained that as cats aged, the barbs on their tongues wore down. Even if they licked themselves regularly, they couldn't do an efficient job grooming because there was nothing to separate the fur. Tangles and mats were just another symptom of old age.

"As for these," Dr. Franck said, studying Dewey's clumped back end, "drastic measures are required. I think we better shave."

When she was done, poor Dewey was fuzzy on one end, naked on the other. He looked like he was wearing a big coat and no pants. A few members of the staff laughed when they saw him, because it was a hilarious sight, but they didn't laugh long. The humiliation on Dewey's face stopped that. He hated it. Just hated it.

He walked away very fast for a few steps, then sat down and tried to hide his rear end. Then he got up, walked quickly away, and sat down again. Start, sit. Start, sit. He finally made it back to his bed, buried his head in his paws, and curled up beneath his favorite toy, Marty Mouse. For days, we found him with his top half sticking out into an aisle and his back end hidden in a bookshelf.

But Dewey's health was no laughing matter. The staff didn't talk about it, but I knew they were worried. They didn't want to be responsible if something happened. Dewey was my cat, and everyone knew it. The last thing they wanted was to have the life of my cat in their hands.

"Don't worry," I told them. "Just do what you think is best for Dewey."

I often traveled out of town on library business. I couldn't promise the staff nothing would happen while I was away, but I told them, "I know this cat. I know when he is healthy, a little sick, and really sick. If he's really sick, trust me, he's going to the vet. I'll do whatever it takes."

Besides, Dewey wasn't sick. He still jumped up and down from the circulation desk, so I knew his arthritis wasn't too bad. His digestion was better than ever. And he still loved company. But it took patience to care for an elderly cat, and frankly, some of the staff didn't think that was their job.

Slowly, as Dewey aged, his support peeled away: first those in town who didn't really like him; then some of the fence-sitters; then a few patrons who only wanted an attractive, active cat; and finally the staff members who didn't want the burden of an elderly cat.

That doesn't mean I wasn't blindsided by the October library board meeting. I was expecting a typical discussion of the state of the library, but the meeting soon turned into a referendum on Dewey. A patron had mentioned he wasn't looking well. Perhaps, the board suggested, we should get him some medical help?

"At his recent checkup," I told them, "Dr. Franck discovered hyperthyroidism. It's just another symptom of age, like his arthritis, his dry skin, and the black age spots on his lips and gums. Dr. Franck prescribed a medication. I rub it in his ear. Dewey has really perked up. And don't worry," I reminded them, "we're paying for the medicine with donations and my own money. Not a single penny of city money is ever spent on Dewey's care."

"Is hyperthyroidism serious?"

"Yes, but it's treatable."

"Will this medicine help his fur?"

"Dullness isn't a disease, it's a function of age, like gray hair on a human." They should understand. There wasn't a head in the room without a few gray hairs.

"What about his weight?"

I explained his diet, from the obsessiveness with which Donna and I changed his cat food to the Arby's Beef 'n' Cheddar sandwiches.

"But he doesn't look good," someone said.

They kept coming back to that. Dewey didn't look good. Dewey was hurting the image of the library. I knew they meant well, but I couldn't understand their thinking. It was true, Dewey didn't look as appealing. Everybody ages. Eighty-year-olds don't look like twenty-year-olds, and they shouldn't. But maybe older people, and older cats, have something to teach us, especially about ourselves.

"Why don't you take Dewey home to live with you? I know he visits you on holidays."

I had thought of that. But I knew Dewey could never be happy living at my house. I was gone too much, and he hated to be alone. He was a public cat. He needed people around him to be happy.

"We've had complaints, Vicki, don't you understand? Our job is to speak for the citizens of this town."

The board seemed ready to say the town didn't want Dewey anymore. I knew that was ridiculous because I saw the community's love for Dewey every day. Maybe the board had received a few complaints, but there had always been complaints. Now, with Dewey not looking his best, the voices were louder. But that didn't mean the town had turned on Dewey. One thing I'd learned over the years was that the people who loved Dewey, who really wanted and needed him, weren't the ones with the loudest voices. They were often the ones with no voices at all.

And even if what the board thought was true, even if the majority of the town had turned its back on Dewey, didn't we nonetheless have the duty to stand by him? Even if only five people cared, wasn't that enough? Even if nobody cared, Dewey loved the town of Spencer. He would always love Spencer. He needed us. We couldn't just toss him out because looking at him, older and weaker, no longer made us proud.

There was another message from the board, too, and it came through loud and clear: Dewey is not your cat. He's the town's cat. We speak for the town, so it's our decision. We know what's best.

I won't argue one fact. Dewey was Spencer's cat. But he was also *my* cat. And finally, in the end, Dewey was *a* cat. At that meeting, I realized that in many people's minds, Dewey had gone from being a flesh-and-blood animal with thoughts and feelings, to being an object that could be owned. Library board members loved Dewey as a cat, but they still couldn't separate the animal from the symbol.

And I have to admit, there was another thought going through my mind. *I'm getting older. My health isn't the best. Are these people going to throw me out, too?*

"I know I am close to Dewey," I told the board. "Maybe you think I love Dewey too much. Maybe you think my love clouds my judgment. But trust me. I'll know when it's time. I've had animals all my life. I've put them down. It's hard, but I can do it. The very last thing I want, the very last thing, is for Dewey to suffer."

A board meeting can be a freight train, and this one pushed me off to the side like a cow on the tracks. Someone suggested a committee to make decisions about Dewey's future. I knew the people on that committee would mean well. I knew they would take their duty seriously and do what they thought best. But I couldn't let that happen. I just couldn't.

194

The board was discussing how many people should be on this Dewey Death Watch Committee when one member, Sue Hitchcock, spoke up. "This is ridiculous," she said. "I can't believe we're even discussing this. Vicki has been at the library for twenty-five years. She's been with Dewey for nineteen years. She knows what she's doing. We should all trust Vicki's judgment."

Thank God for Sue Hitchcock. As soon as she spoke, the train jumped the tracks and the board backed off. "Yes, yes," they muttered, "you're right...too soon, too much...if his condition worsens..."

I was devastated. It stung me to the heart that these people had even suggested taking Dewey away from me. And they could have done it. They had the power. But they didn't. Somehow, we had won a victory: for Dewey, for the library, for the town. For me.

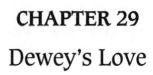

CHAPTER 29

Dewey's Love

In September 2006, just a few weeks before the board meeting where we had talked about Dewey's condition, a program at the library brought in almost a hundred people. I figured Dewey would hide in the staff area, but there he was, mingling as always. He was like a shadow moving among the guests, often unnoticed but somehow there at the end of their hand each time someone reached to pet him. There was a rhythm to his interactions that seemed the most natural and beautiful thing in the world.

After the program, Dewey climbed into his bed above Kay's desk, clearly exhausted. Kay came over and gave him a gentle scratch on the chin. I knew that touch. It was a thank-you, the one you give an old friend after you've watched them across a crowded room and realized how wonderful they are, and how lucky you are to have them in your life. I half expected her to say, "That'll do, cat, that'll do," like the farmer in the movie *Babe*, but Kay left the words unsaid.

Two months later, in early November, Dewey's walk became a bit unsteady. He started peeing excessively, sometimes on the paper outside his litter box, which he had never done before. But he wasn't hiding. He was still jumping up and down from the circulation desk. He still interacted with patrons. He didn't seem to be in pain. I called Dr. Franck, and she advised me just to watch him closely.

Then one morning, just after Thanksgiving, Dewey wasn't waving. All those years, and I could count on one hand the number of times Dewey wasn't waving when I arrived in the morning. Instead he was standing at the front door, just waiting for me. I ushered him to the litter box and gave him his can of cat food. He ate a few bites, then walked with me around the library. I was busy preparing for a trip to Florida, so I left Dewey with the staff for the rest of the morning. As always, he came in while I was working to sniff my air vent and make sure I was safe. The older he got, the more he protected the ones he loved.

At nine-thirty I went out for Dewey's breakfast of the moment, a Hardee's Bacon, Egg and Cheese Biscuit. When I returned, Dewey didn't come running. I figured the deaf old boy didn't hear the door. I found him sleeping on a chair by the circulation desk, so I swung the bag a few times, floating the smell of eggs his way. He flew out of that chair into my office. I put the egg-and-cheese mush on a paper plate, and he ate three or four bites before curling up on my lap.

At ten thirty, Dewey attended Story Hour. As usual, he greeted every child. An eight-year-old girl was sitting on the floor with her legs crossed. Dewey curled up on her legs and went to sleep. She petted him, the other children took turns petting him, everyone was happy. After Story Hour, Dewey crawled into his fur-lined bed in front of the heater, and that's where he was when I left the library at noon. I was going home for lunch, then picking up my dad and driving to Omaha to catch a flight the next morning.

Ten minutes after I got home, the phone rang.

It was Jann, one of our clerks. "Dewey's acting funny."

"What do you mean 'funny'?"

"He's crying and walking funny. And he's trying to hide in the cupboards."

"I'll be right down."

Dewey was hiding under a chair. I picked him up, and he was shaking like the morning I found him. His eyes were big, and I could tell he was in pain. I called the veterinary office. Dr. Franck was out, but her husband, Dr. Beall, was in.

"Come right down," he said.

I wrapped Dewey in his towel. It was a cold day. Dewey snuggled against me immediately.

By the time we arrived at the vet's office, Dewey was down on the floor of my car by the heater, shaking with fear. I cradled him in my arms and held him against my chest. That's when I noticed poop sticking out of his behind.

What a relief! It wasn't serious. It was just poop!

I told Dr. Beall the problem. He took Dewey into the back room to clean him out. Dewey came out wet and cold. He crawled from Dr. Beall's arms into mine and looked up at me with pleading eyes. *Help me.* I could tell something still wasn't right.

Dr. Beall said, "I can feel a mass in his stomach."

"What is it?"

"I don't know. He needs an X-ray."

Ten minutes later, Dr. Beall was back with the results. There was a large tumor in Dewey's stomach, pushing on his kidneys and intestines. That's why he had been peeing more, and it probably accounted for his peeing outside the litter box.

"It wasn't there in September," Dr. Beall said, "which means it's probably an aggressive cancer. But we'd have to do invasive tests to find out for sure."

We stood silently, looking at Dewey. I never suspected the tumor. Never. I knew everything about Dewey, all his thoughts and feelings, but he had kept this one thing hidden from me.

"Is he in pain?"

"Yes, I suspect he is. The mass is growing very fast, so it will only get worse."

"Is there anything you can give him for the pain?"

"No, not really."

I was holding Dewey in my arms, cradling him

like a baby. He hadn't let me carry him that way in sixteen years. Now he wasn't even fighting it. He was just looking at me.

"Do you think he's in constant pain?"

"I can't imagine that he's not."

The conversation was crushing me, flattening me out, making me feel drawn, deflated, tired. I couldn't believe what I was hearing. I had believed Dewey was going to live forever.

I called the library staff and told them Dewey wasn't coming home. Kay was out of town. Joy was off duty. They reached her at Sears, but too late. Several others came down to say good-bye. Instead of going to Dewey, Sharon walked right up and hugged me. Thank you, Sharon, I needed that. Then I hugged Donna and thanked her for loving Dewey so much. Donna was the last to say her good-byes.

Someone said, "I don't know if I want to be here when they put him to sleep."

"That's fine," I said. "I'd rather be alone with him."

Dr. Beall took Dewey into the back room to insert the IV, then brought him back in a fresh blanket and put him in my arms. I talked to Dewey for a few minutes. I told him how much

I loved him, how much he meant to me, how much I didn't want him to suffer. I explained what was happening and why. I rewrapped his blanket to make sure he was comfortable. What more could I offer him than comfort? I cradled him in my arms and rocked back and forth from foot to foot, a habit started when he was a kitten. Dr. Beall gave him the first shot, followed closely by the second.

He said, "I'll check for a heartbeat."

I said, "You don't need to. I can see it in his eyes."

Dewey was gone.

CHAPTER 30

Loving Dewey

For eight days, I didn't read the newspaper. I didn't watch television. I didn't take any phone calls. It was the best possible time to be away in Florida because Dewey's death was hard. Very hard. I broke down on the flight from Omaha and cried all the way to Houston. I cried almost all the way to Florida, too.

Meanwhile, the Spencer radio station devoted their morning show to memories of Dewey. The *Sioux City Journal* ran a lengthy story and obituary. The AP wire picked up the story and sent it around the world. Within hours, news of Dewey's death appeared on the CBS afternoon newsbreak and on MSNBC.

The library started getting calls. If I had been in the library, I would have been stuck answering questions from reporters for days, but nobody else on staff felt comfortable speaking to the media. The library secretary gave a brief statement, which ended up in Dewey's obituary, but that was all. It was enough. Over the next few days, that obituary ran in more than 270 newspapers.

The response from individuals touched by Dewey was equally overwhelming. People in town received calls from friends and relatives all over the country who read about Dewey's death or heard it on a local radio show. One local couple was out of the country and learned the news from a friend in San Francisco, who read about his passing in the *San Francisco Chronicle*.

Admirers set up a vigil in the library. Local businesses sent flowers and gifts. Sharon and Tony's daughter with Down syndrome, Emmy, drew a picture of Dewey. It was two green circles in the middle of the page with lines sticking out in all directions. It was beautiful, and Emmy beamed as I taped it to my office door. That picture was the perfect way for both of us to remember him.

By then, there were letters and cards stacked

four feet high on my desk. I had more than six hundred e-mails about Dewey in my inbox. Many were from people who met him only once but never forgot him. Hundreds of others were from people who never met him.

In the month after his death, I received more than a thousand e-mails about Dewey from all around the world. We heard from a soldier in Iraq who had been touched by Dewey's death despite what he saw there every day—or perhaps because of it. We received a letter from a couple in Connecticut whose son was turning eleven; his birthday wish was to release a balloon to heaven in Dewey's honor.

Many people in town wanted to hold a memorial service. I didn't want a memorial service, but we had to do something. So on a cold Saturday in the middle of December, Dewey's admirers gathered at the library to remember one last time, at least officially, the friend who had had such an impact on their lives. The staff tried to keep it light—I told the story of the bat, Audrey told the story of the lights, Joy remembered the cart rides, Sharon told how Dewey stole the meat out of her sandwich—but despite our best efforts, tears were shed.

Crews from local television stations were filming the event. It was a nice thought, but the cameras seemed out of place. These were private thoughts among friends; we didn't want to share our words with the world. We also realized, as we stood there together, that words couldn't describe our feelings for Dewey. There was no easy way to say how special he was. Finally a local schoolteacher said, "People say what's the big deal, he was just a cat. But that's where they're wrong. Dewey was so much more." Everyone knew exactly what she meant.

The next few days were hard. The staff had cleaned out his bowls and donated his food while I was away, but I had to give away his toys. I had to clean out his shelf: the Vaseline for his hair balls, the brush, the red yarn he had played with all his life. I had to park my car and walk to the library every morning without Dewey waving at me from the front door.

When the staff returned to the library after visiting Dewey for the last time, the space heater he had lain in front of every day wasn't working. Dewey had been lying in front of it that very morning, and it had been working fine. It was as if his death had taken away its reason to heat.

Can a malfunctioning piece of equipment break your heart? It was six weeks before I could even think about having that heater repaired.

I had Dewey cremated with one of his favorite toys, Marty Mouse, so he wouldn't be alone. The crematorium offered a free wooden box and bronze plaque, but I didn't want them. Dewey came back to his library in a plain plastic container inside a blue velvet bag. I put the container on a shelf in my office and went back to work.

A week after his memorial service, I came out of my office a half hour before the library opened, long before any patrons arrived, and told Kay, "It's time."

It was December, another brutally cold Iowa morning. Just like Dewey's first morning, and so many in between. It was close to the shortest day of the year, and the sun wasn't yet up. The sky was still deep blue, almost purple, and there was no traffic on the roads. The only sound was the cold wind whipping down the streets and out over the barren cornfields.

We moved some rocks in the little garden in front of the library, looking for a place where the ground wasn't completely frozen. But the whole earth was frosted, and it took a while for Kay to dig the hole. The sun was peeking over the buildings on the far side of the parking lot by the time I placed the remains of my friend in the ground and said simply, "You're always with us, Dewey. This is your home."

Then Kay dropped in the first shovelful of dirt, burying Dewey's ashes forever outside the window of the children's library, at the foot of the beautiful statue of a mother reading a book to her child. As Kay moved the stones back over Dewey's final resting place, I looked up and saw the rest of the library staff in the window, silently watching us.

EPILOGUE

Dewey's Legacy

Not much seems to change in northwest Iowa. Spencer has a new mayor, a new drugstore, and a new plastic surgeon, but it's still the same old town. The Spencer Public Library rolls on, even without its library cat. Not that people didn't try to change that fact. After Dewey's death, the library had almost a hundred offers for new cats. We had offers from as far away as Texas. The cats were cute, and most had touching survival stories, but there was no enthusiasm to take one. We couldn't simply replace Dewey with another cat. You can't bring back the past.

Instead, the memories of Dewey live on: At the library, where his portrait hangs beside the front door above a bronze plaque that tells his story;

with the children who knew him and will talk about him with their own children and grand-children; and even in this book. After all, that's why I wrote it. For Dewey.

A few years ago, Spencer commissioned a public art installation to serve as both a state-ment about our values and an entry point to our historic downtown. Two ceramic tile mosaic artists spent a year in the area, talking with us, studying our history, and observing our way of life. More than 570 residents, from young chil-dren to grandparents, consulted with the art-ists. The result is a mosaic sculpture called *The Gathering: Of Time, of Land, of Many Hands.*

The Gathering is composed of four decora-tive pillars and three pictorial walls. The south wall is called "The Story of the Land." It is a farm scene featuring corn and pigs, a woman hanging quilts on a clothesline, and a train. The north wall is "The Story of Outdoor Recreation." It focuses on our parks, the fairgrounds on the northwest edge of town, and the nearby lakes. The west wall is "The Story of Spencer." It shows three generations gathering at Grandma's house, the town battling the fire, and a woman making a pot, a metaphor for shaping the future. Just slightly to the left of center, in the upper half of the scene, is an orange cat sitting on the open pages of a library book. The image is based on artwork submitted by a child.

The story of Spencer. Dewey is a part of it: now and forever.

For me, though, the memories are more personal. I remember the little kitten, so dirty and scared, who I lifted out of the book drop that freezing Monday morning. I remember the way he ate rubber bands. The way he rode on the book cart, with all his feet hanging down. I remember hide-and-seek late at night, the touch of his chin on my arm, and all those mornings he waved at me from the front door and my heart soared right out of my chest with joy.

I remember Dewey's last Christmas. My daughter Jodi and her husband Scott stayed at my house. They had twins, Nathan and Hannah, a year and a half old. Hannah and Nathan would toddle up and pet Dewey all over.

Grandpa Dew was cautious around toddlers. In the library, he slunk away when they tried to approach him. But he sat with the twins, even when they petted him the wrong way and messed up his fur. Hannah kissed him a hundred times;

Nathan accidentally knocked him on the head. One afternoon, Hannah poked Dewey in the face while trying to pet him. Dewey didn't even flinch. This was my grandchild. This was Jodi's child. Dewey loved us, so he loved Hannah, too.

Find your place. Be happy with what you have. Treat everyone well. Live a good life. It isn't about material things; it's about love.

Those are the lessons Dewey taught me. But he also taught me something else: you never know when you'll fall in love.

I had decided, when Dewey died, not to get another cat. I had loved Dewey with all my heart, and he had loved me in the same way. It wouldn't be fair to expect that of another cat. The poor animal would always be compared to Dewey, and how could it possibly compete?

Then, two years later, on another bitterly cold Iowa morning, a friend of mine saw a truck swerve suddenly on an icy road in downtown Spencer. She thought there was a clump of ice or snow in the road, so she slowed down. Then she saw the clump move. It was a scared little kitten, shivering in the cold with ice and twigs matted in its fur. My friend took the kitten to her office and gave him a bath, then brought him to the library.

As soon as I saw the little kitten, my heart leaped. It was like seeing Dewey again that first morning in the library drop box: so tiny, so helpless, so wonderfully, beautifully ginger orange. The new kitten had green eyes instead of Dewey's gorgeous gold, and his tail was stubby and short, but otherwise... he was so much like Dewey. Even his long fur and magnificent ruff of neck hair looked like the Dew.

I picked the kitten up and cradled him in my lap. He looked me in the eye and began to purr. Just like with Dewey that first morning, I melted. This was meant to be. Within an hour, the kitten was on his way to my house to live with me.

That night, I mentioned the new kitten on Dewey's website, www.deweyreadmorebooks.com. I was worried Dewey's fans might be disappointed; after all, they loved him, too. Instead, a boy named Cody wrote back to suggest that, since I was turning a new page in my life, I name the kitten Page.

Cody was right. I was turning a new page in my life. I was moving on, starting a new adventure, writing the first words of a new story in the great big book of my life.

That doesn't mean I will ever forget Dewey. He will always be part of me; he will always live in my heart. But Page Turner (my new cat's full name)...he makes me laugh really, really hard. And when he does that, I know everything in the world is all right.